Creativity and Abundance:
Claiming Your Power and Worth

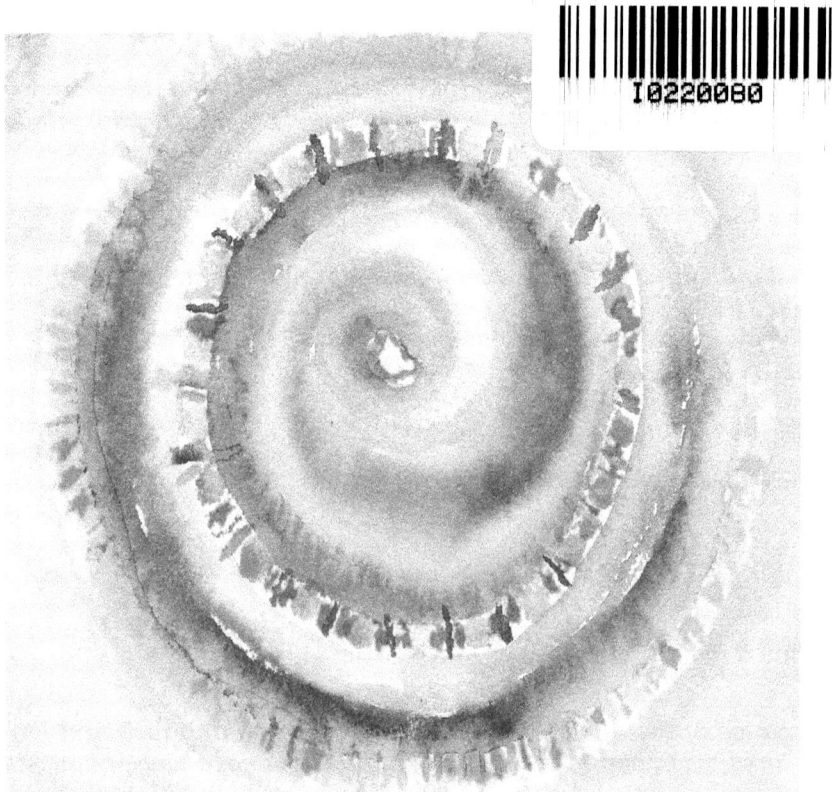

Antoinette Spurrier

*You are a creator of possibilities and an adventurer on a journey.
Your power of intention, imagination, affirmation and your capacity
to dream are your tools to create a life of true happiness aligned
with your higher self.*

© 2012 by Antoinette Spurrier. All rights reserved.

No part of this book may be reproduced, stored in a retrieval system, or transmitted by any means without the written permission of the author.

First published by Antoinette Spurrier through Lightening Source, July 2012

ISBN: 978-0-9856857-0-6 (hc)

ISBN: 978-0-9856857-1-3 (sc)

ISBN: 978-0-9856857-2-0 (ebk)

Library of Congress Control Number: 2012912364

Printed in the United States of America

Because of the dynamic nature of the Internet, any web addresses or links contained in this book may have changed since publication and may no longer be valid. The views expressed in this work are solely those of the author and do not necessarily reflect the views of the publisher, and the publisher hereby disclaims any responsibility for them.

Dedication

This book is dedicated to my mother, Yvonne, who has been my life-long best friend, and to John McLaurin who personified eternal friendship.

Table of Contents

Introduction   1

Chapter One: *Cultivating Creativity*   4

Chapter Two:
Deservedness and How to Feel It   52

Chapter Three:
Abundance and Prosperity   83

Acknowledgements

Collaborators:

Andrew Freedman
Editor, graph maker, friend and preserver of the intention. Andrew was the original inspiration for a mini-book series evolving from *Deliberate Happiness*.

Jacqui Freedman
Artistic contributor who manages to capture Spirit and Nature in her light-filled watercolors that grace the front and back cover of this book. Her work is available at Jacquifree@yahoo.com.

Heidi Hall
Co-editor of the primary *Deliberate Happiness* book. This edition, *Creativity and Abundance: Claiming Your Power and Worth*, is also graced by her inspirational input.

Becky Lawton
Initial contributor and administrative assistant for *Deliberate Happiness*.

Mark Murphy, aka Mr. Creativity.
Provider of multi-faceted contributions that helped make this book a reality.

Deborah Probst Kayes
Proofreader, coordinator and multi-tasker with extraordinary tenacity, patience and loyalty.

Suresh Ramaswamy
Creative website master for www.FieldsOfLight.com.

Ann Summa and Jeffrey Spurrier
Providers of proofreading and formatting expertise, as well as moral support.

Anne Marie Welsh
Co-editor and dynamic catalyst for the birthing process of *Creativity and Abundance: Claiming Your Power and Worth*. The "Book Doc" has allowed the creativity to shine abundantly.

Contributors:

Family and friends who have provided love and moral support in magnanimous ways.

The Foundation for Spiritual and Personal Empowerment that provided the funding resources for the printing and distribution of the Deliberate Happiness book series.

Please refer to FieldsOfLight.com for more information.

Special Mention:

Susann and Richard Fishman
Deirdre Maher and Lou Bewersdorf
Wayne Mantyla
Geoffrey and Sandra Mavis
Patrick McNabb and Catherine Helm
Dr. Carl and Chris Murphy
Lisa Janicek Scurr and Ron Scurr

Introduction

To the Reader,

Creativity and Abundance: Claiming Your Power and Worth is the third installment in my series that began with *Deliberate Happiness*. This shorter work distills several chapters of the main book into a coherent series of discussions and practical exercises to ignite your creativity, confront and remove deservedness issues and thus help lead you toward a life of abundance and prosperity.

My desire is to inspire powerful transformation. This allows you to tap into your own consciousness and creativity. Then, through a process of introspection and practice, you may bring about fundamental changes in your sense of deservedness and thus allow yourself to manifest abundance and prosperity in your life and work. When properly applied, spiritual principles and techniques, including affirmations and meditation, can lead to greater personal and spiritual empowerment. I thus invite you to become a Co-Creator with the Divine in reflection and action. Now is the time to claim your power and abundance.

The full-length *Deliberate Happiness* offers a detailed analysis of the background to these practices and an explanation of the natural patterns and scientific laws governing psychological and spiritual growth. In this smaller volume, I focus on techniques and ideas that, with patience and persistence, will stoke the fires of your creativity and help remove any deservedness issues that thwart your full expression and manifestation of abundance. These techniques include:

- Spiritual practices, such as meditation, visualizations, journaling, introspection and especially affirmations, energized by the application of will.
- A definition of success, health and wealth that focuses beyond the material to a deeper awareness of our Divine nature.

- Techniques to uproot negative self-talk and alter long-standing feelings of worthlessness that sabotage creativity, love, happiness and manifesting abundance.
- A realistic focus on the power of affirmations to help overcome negative thoughts and behaviors which confront us when we seek to express our creative natures.

My intention is to assist you in claiming the most of yourself through self-understanding and proven techniques in personal transformation. As you better understand spiritual law and these techniques, you will become a Co-Creator with the source of all creation. I use a number of terms which some readers may not be familiar with. Please refer to the glossary for maximum benefit.

I discovered these spiritual techniques and practices through first hand experience. Trained in the field of psychology with an emphasis in family counseling and a specialty in treating chemical dependency, my professional life was dramatically interrupted by the onset of a life-threatening, catastrophic illness that challenged me to confront a total upheaval of my beliefs, health and previous capacities.

After surviving continuing medical challenges, I entered into a period of profound personal change that awakened me to a spiritual layer of reality and led on to the evolution of a new and much larger spiritual perspective. I developed an interest in meditation, affirmations and visualization as healing modalities and as tools of growth and empowerment. Each of this book's major chapters ends with suggested affirmations relating to the chapter's theme.

As a spiritual counselor, I have shared these discoveries and approaches with many others, and have seen their profound impact upon those who practice them with sincere belief, patience, persistence and dedication.

Creativity is your birthright; when you remove obstacles to viewing yourself as a Co-Creator with the Divine, you will better be able to express your own uniqueness and manifest abundance and prosperity, eventually returning to your natural state of happiness and joy. You have the inherent power and worth to create more deliberate happiness.

Congratulations on taking this first step!

Antoinette Spurrier
San Diego, California
Spring, 2012

Chapter One

Cultivating Creativity

You are invited to awaken your true nature and to express yourself fully in every way, every day as a dynamic co-creator with the Divine.

We were born out of the vision of God. The Creator of all instilled within us the power of creativity itself as our spiritual birthright. Our conditions and circumstances are precisely perfect to call us to self-awakening. The divinity that is within desires to co-create with us.

Key topics addressed in this chapter:

- Creativity is not a specific talent, finite and limited in origin. We all possess the spark of creativity within.
- Creativity is part of our spiritual nature, not an attribute of personality. With greater awareness of our spiritual nature, we activate the creative force itself.
- Creativity may be further accessed by a more harmonious alignment between the Limited Self and the Eternal Self.
- Creativity may be harnessed by using meditation, visualization, and affirmations, among other techniques. Affirmations can dramatically increase our efforts to expand our awareness of the creative force and our Eternal Self.

Creativity is Infinite

Creativity is not an attribute of personality, nor is it limited to a certain type of artistic person. Creativity is intrinsically tied to our spiritual nature and ultimately to our feelings of happiness. We do not "acquire" it. We simply need to activate that which is already present within. The spark of creativity that ignites the stars, forms universes, and gives color to the flowers, is within us as well. It makes us feel alive, connected to our human family, to nature, beauty and the cosmos. Creativity provides the deepest sense of joy and well-being.

At times in our lives creative effort may seem out of reach. We may cast a longing gaze at the artists of the world thinking we are missing the creative "gene" that was their endowment. Why do some people seem to have greater creative ability than others? If we have it, why haven't we manifested it in our lives?

Whether we experience its presence or not, the seed of creativity *is* within. It is part of the cosmic energy of the universe itself, and thus the very origin of our divine nature. We have the power to tap into and access the expansive flow of creation at any time. Expanding our creative aspect within is a spiritual opportunity and a divine promise.

Messages from our families, our culture, even our own experiences may have led us to mistaken ideas about our creative capacity.

Examples of false ideas about creativity:

- I am not a creative person.
- My creativity is limited.
- I don't have any special creative talents.
- I am not an artist, writer, musician, etc.
- It's too late for me to become creative.
- People are either born creative or they're not.
- I can't be creative and also make money.
- I don't know how to access, or unlock, my creativity.
- I need to be practical and forget creative fulfillment in my life.
- Creativity is impractical and not marketable.
- My creativity is not worthwhile to pursue.
- Creativity is limited and finite, therefore accessible only to a few.
- Creativity cannot be expressed through me, for I am an inferior channel.

Any of these negative ideas can become circular, denying the powerful truth of our innate creativity and our superior status as a channel of inspiration, beauty, and artistry. We must unlock our creativity by changing our thoughts and self-definition.

What is Creativity?

Creativity is our true nature; blocks are an unnatural thwarting of a process at once as normal and as miraculous as the blossoming of a flower at the end of a slender green stem.

Julia Cameron, *The Artist's Way*

Creativity is often viewed from too narrow a perspective. We may think of it as simply an attribute of personality, or link it only to specific talents or abilities: "Others are creative; I am not." When we view creativity only as expressed through specific talents, we further minimize it by claiming that those talents are impractical.

Creativity can never have narrow constraints or definitions because it is a part of All that Is. It is woven into the very atoms. Every aspect of life springs forth out of the fullness of creativity. As we expand our definition of ourselves as a profound part of creation, we open to infinite possibilities. We begin to see ourselves as creative beings with unique and potent ways of expressing life, personality, talents, insights, and intuition. As we harness our imagination and ride it into the heavenly realm, we no longer see ourselves as mere finite expressions of a physical being limited by the body.

In truth, our finite form came from the act of creation. The infinite part of us has never been limited. This understanding frees us to be intentional co-creators with Life itself. In her book *The Zen of Creative Painting,* author Jeanne Carbonetti writes, "Creativity is a mystery. That's the great secret to unearthing its treasures. For what you seek to explore and to fathom is really yourself. From the moment we are born, our birthright is to play with the great creative process that is our life."

Creativity is not about acquisition, but about unleashing our inherent power

Creativity is the breath of the gods, giving life, joy, and inspiration to our human existence. Creativity bridges heaven and earth. When we are in tune with our creative nature, we step into another dimension. We explore the heights and depths of our spiritual nature.

We should periodically take stock of our thoughts on creativity. Do we see ourselves as limited, lacking creative talents and personality attributes? Can we identify the origin of these self-assessments? Can we remember specific messages about our creative insufficiencies?

The words and attitudes of others, as well as the successes and disappointments of others, have impacted all of us. Can we recollect any experiences that affected how we see our creativity? Was creativity encouraged or discouraged when we were children?

Regardless of the messages we received as children, it is never too late to tap into this dynamo within. The brilliant painter, Henry Matisse, succinctly put it this way: "Creativity takes courage." It takes courage to overcome self-doubt, to try new things, to face our vulnerabilities and to embark on new adventures. Creative effort begins with intention. All journeys begin with a focused aim, followed by will-directed activity.

Tools that Enhance Creativity

Listed below are principles and practices by which we open to our creativity. Consciousness exploration, such as examining habitual patterns of thought, is key to accessing our natural creative abilities.

- **Imagination** – Examine the role imagination and intuition play in your life at present.
- **Self permission** - Open yourself to change and release fear of change.
- **Dynamic intention** – Trust the power within to create what you intend.
- **Dynamic willpower** – The energized thrust of creative potency.
- **Visualization** of yourself as a creative being doing creative acts and arriving at creative solutions.
- **Affirmations** which assert your potency as creator of your destiny.
- **Meditation** which emphasizes interiorized consciousness.

We all approach our creativity in different ways. For some, walking through nature inspires the inner muse; for others, meditation or listening to music may provide the entry. Creativity may speak to us in silence or when visiting places of beauty, such as the Louvre. The well known poet, David Whyte, spoke of accessing creativity through a deep inner conversation with ourselves: "You've got to find that contact point as an individual. Ask the question, "Where am I interested? Where, in a very short time, do I become passionate once I've opened up that initial interest? What do I have energy for? And will I have faith to actually spend enough time to open up that door into what to begin with is a new territory, but eventually becomes my new home?"

Mahatma Gandhi also reminds us that we have the answers within: "Everyone who wills can hear the inner Voice. It is within all."

Tuning in to this inner voice and hearing its message will bring forth the deeper clarity we are seeking. Remember that creative expression has no limitation. It is what moves us uniquely. What we feel, and how we are moved, will be unlike anyone else's way. All new inventions began with the spark of unique creativity – bringing something into the world that no one had dreamed of before.

Introspection Exercise

- List five experiences during which you felt, or demonstrated, some form of creativity, even if you were a child at the time. This may include areas of expression such as a poem, a song, a drawing, or perhaps a creative idea or notion.
- List comments that you remember being said about how someone else saw your creative talents.
- Did you hear discouraging or encouraging statements about your creative interests or attempts? Which statements were predominant?
- Did you internalize any of these ideas, thoughts, or experiences? If so, which ones?
- Did anyone inspire or restrict your passionate interest in any area of specific creative endeavor? If so, how?

Definitive statements and assessments about our creative expression have a potent effect on us, for better or for worse. Professor of Art Education David London wrote, "All statements marking good and bad, like and dislike, in some fashion damage our spirit and consequently lead us to pull on our defensive armor. This is a terribly steep price to pay for what is actually desired in the exchange: increased capacity for breadth of imagination and clarity of expression." If we lacked encouragement, especially in our formative years, there is a good chance our creativity was stunted.

Whatever detrimental effects there may be from our past, however stymied we may feel in our creative endeavors, *we can change*. To desire more creativity is a start. If we find ourselves reflecting on returning to an area of creative interest, that is movement. As we back that reflection with focused intention, it will eventually come to pass. Creativity is our birthright and is always there for us, however obscured it may be.

Make a Dream List

Make a dream list of those creative areas that you would like to expand. After you complete the list, prioritize the top two areas. Do not hesitate to list interests in which you have had no previous experience. If you have always wanted to play a musical instrument, put it down even if you feel intimidated by the prospect. How can you give yourself permission to try a new area in which you have not built confidence? How will you build confidence by refusing to begin and to try?

Suggestions for creating your dream list:

1. **Unleash your imagination**: Give yourself permission to name your dreams, identify your hopes, desires and what

you believe will make you happy. Remember, creativity has no limits.

2. **Identify areas of creative interest:** What interested you as a child? Were you drawn to color, or fantasy, dance or mechanics? Be sure not to censor any area because you believe it's impractical.
3. **Creativity is an experiment in expanding awareness**: Select a couple of areas in which you desire to begin creative exploration.
4. **As we see ourselves, so we become**: Imagine yourself successfully, joyously working in the areas of interest you just identified. As we imagine, we cast a blueprint of the future which has the power to become manifest.
5. **Set aside time**: Structure some time to begin exploring and working with these interests. Schedule an appointment with yourself and write it down! Prioritize your appointments with yourself as you begin to visit with more of your creativity.
6. **Dynamic intention:** With focused intention, pursue techniques of visualization and affirmations that emphasize your creativity.
7. **Integrate creativity into daily life:** Let creativity enliven your business, family life, romantic and spiritual life. Every aspect of life can benefit from the creative flair from within.

Giving Ourselves Permission to Change

Have you ever wondered what gets in the way of claiming our own happiness? If happiness is so important, why isn't it easier to attain? One reason is that the Limited Self—the you that is finite, mortal and living in the material world—becomes attached to its own limitation. Human nature tends to hold on to what is familiar, even if it is confining or brings discontent. Before any change can happen, we must give ourselves permission to release those parts of us that resist change. We must embrace our worthiness to succeed. Resistance to new endeavors clips the wings upon which our creativity soars heaven-bound.

To understand our resistance to change we first must understand our own dual nature as both a Limited Self and an Eternal Self. These selves are in frequent communication and yet function in nearly opposite ways. This is not an abstract philosophical quandary; it is a reality. The Limited Self is identified and bound by a person's physical form, mind, feelings and culture. The other, the Eternal Self, expresses our spiritual nature, our true unchangeable essence.

The Limited Self has four aspects: our biological nature, operating in the physical dimension; our psychological layers of mental consciousness, operating within a social context; our beliefs and life experiences, operating within our environment and culture; and our imagination that can interpret and assign meaning to our experiences. The Limited Self may feel compartmentalized, incorrectly interpreting experiences and events, convinced of that which we wrongly imagine ourselves to be: body identified and impermanent.

Our other Self, the expansive Eternal Self, is our true spiritual nature, its state of consciousness is transcendent joy. That Self, our soul nature, is aware of the actions of the Limited Self and manifests in subtle ways as an expression of who we truly are. Freely exercising our creativity can create a bridge linking Limited and Eternal, creating alignment and harmonious cooperation between them. Exercising our creative imaginations can put us in touch with the Divine Flow of creativity, actually making us co-Creators with the Divine.

By giving ourselves permission to change, imagination will stir and gain momentum to move along new lines. The commitment to change and the desire to open to our creativity must come together in harmonious alignment in order for there to be the effective thrust of will.

Will is the energetic spark that ignites all our worthy endeavors. To desire without energy, to desire without vision, is to invite stagnation and reduce the possibilities of full claiming. We must first place our intention upon our creative desires. Placing intention will begin to stir dynamic will-based energy. Intention is our broadcast to the Divine and to the divinity within. This broadcast will awaken us, and summon immediate response from the universal divine energy that is ever supporting our endeavors. Our unfolding and expansion is of vital interest to the Source of all. The creative force, itself, is universal. The way in which we shape it will remain our individualized expression.

Becoming Fearless

What are our fears around undertaking new creative efforts? We should ask ourselves, "What is the worst thing that can happen to me if I try and do not succeed?" We have not run out of life. We are redefining ourselves as risk-takers. Learning to take risks expands access to our creative nature. Change comes from taking action in spite of fear. Creativity comes by taking the first step in redefining ourselves as creative beings.

Once we have given ourselves permission to change, we will still need to keep reminding ourselves of our commitment. As we embrace positive change wholeheartedly, we begin a process that opens us to the Universal Flow. We find ourselves supported by powerful forces of the Universe. We thereby ignite the creative force within, ablaze with new possibilities. We become a magnet of creativity, a channel and a pathway of inspiration and inventiveness. Our true artistry is born.

The door to creativity remains always open, but no one can walk through it for us. Regardless of our particular habits, feelings of unworthiness, lack of self confidence or negative self talk, if we continue to make the effort, we will be victorious. Be patient! If the pace of your progress disappoints you, keep on anyway.

History is filled with inspiring examples of artists who persevered despite the greatest odds. In 1913 when Igor Stravinsky debuted his now famous *Rite of Spring*, audiences rioted, the noise overwhelming the orchestra. Yet this very work assured his place in musical history by changing the way composers in the 20th century thought about music. Today Monet's paintings sell for millions of dollars and hang in some of the most prestigious institutions in the world. Yet during his own time, his work was mocked and rejected by the artistic elite, the Paris Salon. Monet kept at his impressionist style, which caught on and became a starting point for major changes to art that ushered in the modern era.

Had either Stravinsky or Monet lacked the patience to persevere, or succumbed to negative or self-defeating thoughts, the world would never have been graced with their unique artistic expression. Their examples, and many others, should encourage us in our own efforts to free ourselves from self doubt. Much like the onion that is formed in layers, the odorous layers of false thoughts must be peeled away, one by one, in order to shed our misconceptions. All acts of change and empowerment begin with giving ourselves permission to change, redefine, and imagine.

Creativity and Imagination

Creativity and imagination are synergistic. Imagination inspires creativity and forms the seed thoughts of the light which are then cultivated into other expressions of creativity. *Creativity begets more creativity.* The more we unleash its latent power, the more we have. The more we have, the more unbounded is its expression in our lives.

To imagine is to cast the image into a light form by using our minds. The more that image is retraced by the imagination, the greater the power of imagining. The more we exercise imagination, the greater the potential for creating seed thoughts and direct creative expressions.

To imagine means that we are a painter in the light, and a sculptor and form maker in the light. Nothing will materialize in form without the light image being cast first. The source of that imagination is Spirit -- a vast sea of Spirit that is limitless. As we use our mental abilities in this way, we are remaking our life, accessing creative power, and unlocking the potency and the potential of who we are.

Creativity and Love

An energized heart is a creative heart. An energized heart is expansive in loving. It increases its capacity by the art of loving. Stagnation of energy in the heart center diminishes the creative flow. If we would expand our creativity, we must increase our loving.

To live in the love vibration is to activate the heart center. The heart expands by the act of giving. It is out of love and union that creativity expresses itself in the highest way with the conception of a child. From seed energy, the embryo is formed, and from the embryo, the baby is born. When love is in the heart of the mother and father, that very vibration enters into the seed (the ovum/sperm). The life forming is impregnated by the vibration of love generated from the heart center itself. Through love, creation occurs. Through continuous loving, creation is enhanced.

Love ignites passion, which is expansive participation with Spirit. To encourage greater creativity in life, love more, give more, and serve more, selflessly. This loving, giving, and serving will further create an alignment between the limited, material parts of our nature and our eternal, spiritual selves. The greater the alignment between these two parts of our nature, the more we experience congruency with our deeper nature and with the flow of life itself. This is the key to manifesting our dreams. All of these elements are involved in the idea of an energized heart. Loving is the key to this expansion.

One method of activating the heart center is to concentrate on the spine and consciously bring energy from the lower section of the spinal column near the coccyx, up toward the dorsal area of the spine opposite the heart. Once the energy has been centered in the heart center, visualize the concentration of white light before consciously broadcasting the energized feeling outward in expanding waves of love. Adherents of many spiritual paths use this technique to develop love and compassion.

A second way of achieving an energized heart is to imagine dropping the chattering mind down into the light at the heart center. Many yoga traditions adopt this visualization as a way of stilling the fluctuations of the mind so that the body and spirit can achieve stillness, and in that stillness, open the creative channel. Author, editor and yoga instructor Anne Marie Welsh (www.annemariewelsh.com) uses this and other visualization techniques in her Transformational Yoga for Writers workshops and retreats to help writers focus and stay in the flow of inspiration without interference from the mind and its negative self-judgments.

Creativity: The Limited Self and the Eternal Self

If we believe creativity is primarily an expression of the finite, Limited Self, then creativity, by its nature, is limited. This narrow vantage point ties us to our physical, psychological identity in the material world. From the perspective of the Limited Self, not only is supply limited, but manifestation is finite and restricted. Belief in finite restriction significantly stunts the expression of creativity. This perspective narrows us because it encases us in a view that we are only a biological being, or a personality. This is not true of who we are and who we are becoming.

For the Limited Self, creativity combines skill sets, specific abilities, and/or attributes. If we measure our personal worthiness in this way, we will perceive limitations in our capacity to express creativity. Our creativity then becomes tied to faulty self-definitions and issues of deservedness.

Creativity and the Eternal Self

Creativity, as viewed from the vantage point of the Eternal Self, is another thing entirely. We not only possess, but are a powerhouse that has access to the dynamic force of creation itself. The nature of the Eternal Self is beyond any limit whatsoever.

From the perspective of the Eternal Self, we know our lineage flows from the Creator of all. We are intrinsically connected to everything we could ever want or need in our creative journey. The inward diving into those still waters of Spirit will harvest the pearls of that Self in all their luminous glory. In the silence, creativity flows. In the imagination, creativity flourishes. In will-directed activity, creativity manifests.

As we increase the alignment within ourselves, the Limited and Eternal Selves enter into harmony and thus, we become more authentic. There is no "pretend" or presumption. The ego-based personality falls away, giving birth to a more refined, integrated being. We sense a new centeredness within our core nature—the soul—which naturally aligns and participates with the limitless universe and the power and force of creation itself.

The Passion of Suffering versus the Passion of Joy

Whatever the form of artistic expression, whether it is painting, music, writing, poetry, dance, etc., many believe that suffering is necessary for creation. This popular misconception—that artistic expression requires nearly unbearable sacrifice and suffering—has been fueled by images of tormented artists throughout history as well as in contemporary culture. True artistic passion can exist in suffering. Yet while some individuals in their suffering have managed to create great art, deep and great suffering rarely translates into enduring artistic works. Artistic passion can also exist in divine expression and joy, a state from which lasting work is more likely to emerge.

Neither suffering nor joy are static or stationary, but move as energy lines in creation. They also generate either a negative flow of energy or a positive flow of energy in the universal flow. How we feel passion, with either suffering or joy, creates in us a legacy of consciousness habits. If we wish our artistic expression to emanate from joy, then we should develop a greater alignment with the Eternal Self.

For some, of course, art flows naturally out of a deep sense of joy, love, abundance and the desire to express and share their creative gifts. Others may not agree that a joy-filled consciousness can inspire the essence of deeply felt art. However, passion is the unifying experience which exists in creation and in destruction. Passion exists in polarity. Where and how we channel that passion will determine, to some degree, how we move with those lines of energy. Remember that these moving lines of energy also have the power of magnetism and attraction. The movement of energy continues to operate by the law of attraction, whether it is criticized, rejected, exalted or embraced. How we participate in our passion brings forth new lines of magnetic attraction.

A kind of happiness may be based upon self-indulgence of the Limited Self. Joy, on the other hand, is the domain of the Eternal Self. Except with a Christ-like figure of true spiritual stature, suffering cannot uplift the consciousness of others or oneself. Suffering, without higher spiritual purpose or enlightenment, can become an invitation for others to join us in misery.

The passion of joy also has great power to emanate from and continue resonating within the universe itself. The passion of suffering also has the power to emanate, but that emanation ties us to a negative flow of energy. With an effort to access more of our joy-filled nature, we can tap into and experience creativity to the fullest. Whether we desire to express and capture aspects of passion associated with suffering or with expansive joy is up to us —both are available.

Those who desire greater self-integration will discover that the universe is on tap for our wildest dreams. Creativity is not limited to our earthly experiences, but instead contains the primordial energy of all experience, all passion, and all joy. The Source of creativity is within us, brimming over with possibilities and always ready to support, encourage and inspire us. Aligned with it, our discoveries are transcendent and illuminating. We were born to contribute. We were born to be creators.

Creativity: We unleash it— we don't acquire it

Our real power is not the acquisition of talent or creativity, but the unlocking and unleashing of the dormant power of the Creator within. This occurs when we open to our divine nature as creative beings. We express more creativity when we:
- Claim our creativity as our birthright.
- Explore our dreams and inspirations.
- Make time for creative endeavors.
- Journal as a creative tool. (A good resource is *The Artists' Way* by Julia Cameron.)
- Become more aware/conscious of what holds us back and work on reversing those thoughts/behaviors.
- Visualize and affirm creativity.

Exploring our Dreams as Sources of Inspiration and Creativity

No dream can come into manifestation without first allowing ourselves to dream. What are our most precious dreams? What are the hopes and desires that we want to experience? The dreams we dream in our waking state are the hopes and desires that we long to achieve. Explore these ideas, feelings, desires and urges.

Are there new areas of creative expression that we are curious about? No image can take form without the imagination. No energy can be moved forward by sheer willpower alone. We must first have the framework for it. Let us see ourselves as powerful creators capable of recasting old roles and manufacturing new mental movie scripts in which we are more joyous, happy, and creatively expressive.

To do this, invite imagination to a new level. Envision that you are an actor creating the script of your life on the big screen. Mentally cast yourself in a creative role. What does that part look like? Does it involve a high level of performance with a specific skill? Or do you see the actor exhibiting definite attributes? Is there a specific talent, or area of mastery that you have long desired to explore, exhibit, or perform? Let your imagination open fully, without entertaining any limitation. What would your life look like if you were absolutely assured of success?

To increase your capacity to imagine, practice visualizing the various roles. Combining the visualization with the successful emotional feeling state will intensify the experience. Giving form to dreams, making them concrete in your imagination, and feeling the experience *as if it were real*, will further stimulate the creative process. The time to begin is now. We must not only give ourselves permission to dream, but cast ourselves as the star performer in our personalized dream-script.

Write down your thoughts and feelings in a journal reserved specifically for exploring your dreams. How can we explore what dreams are worth pursuing, if we are not fully clear about what they are? No dream or desire can materialize without an initial seed thought. That seed thought must be supported by intention and will-based energy.

If We are to Dream our Dreams, Avoid Mind-Altering Chemicals

Many habitual users of substances believe that their hopes, desires, and dreams, are more powerful and more imaginative because of the use of chemicals, drugs, or marijuana.

However, chemicals that may stimulate the flow of ideas can also paralyze the power of will to move those ideas forward. Such substances hamper the development of self-discipline. They impair the focus and direction of the energy needed to activate will power.

Creativity requires the combination of inspiration and imagination with will-based activity. At some point, thoughts and ideas must be propelled forward by concentration and dynamic will. No matter how beautiful the automobile, it will not go far without a fully functioning engine. Marijuana, among other substances, kills initiative, drive, and action. It dulls ambition and seduces the user into simply dreaming the dreams with no follow through in action or production.

There are no shortcuts in the effort to materialize a creative life. The human imagination is not dependent upon chemicals for its origin because God's thoughts stir in the sea of Spirit and creation. Our focused intention allows us to ride the waves of inspiration and imagination in that limitless sea. Chemicals may promise oceanic experiences, but actually bind and tie us to the shores of stagnation for they are an effort to stimulate that which is not in need of stimulation. Regular use of mind-altering substances provides the illusion of creating experiences without actualizing them in everyday life.

An interiorized consciousness—achieved through quality meditation techniques outlined at the end of this chapter—expands our consciousness. Sedation of consciousness is not the same as interiorizing of consciousness. Sedation dwarfs knowing. It can also create dependence upon the substance, if not chemically, then psychologically. Meditation, with quality techniques, is a superior pathway to knowing and experiencing our creativity.

Dreams During the Sleep State Enhance Creativity

The pre-sleep state and actual dream experiences are powerful tools to enhance the creative journey.

- Our dream life is positive proof of the power of our imagination and our inherent creativity. Our "storytelling" and image-making while asleep exhibit unbounded creativity. This should encourage us to re-define ourselves as imaginative, inspired, and creative.
- Our dream life may also function as a spiritual compass. The Eternal Self may use the language and symbols of dreams to inspire us toward self-alignment and self-knowing, thus increasing our ability to examine our wants/needs/desires with more honesty and clarity. The Eternal Self frequently sends messages to the Limited Self about what is needed to have a deeper connection with self, and with Spirit. The Eternal Self encourages the consciousness toward greater joy, self-knowing, and love.
- Our dreams mirror our habits of consciousness and our deepest attitudes. We project our habits of mind into our dream patterns, which then become a reflective mirror.
- Pre-sleep suggestions can allow the cycle of dreaming and sleep to improve our ability to engage in positive behaviors when awake. Pre-sleep suggestions can incubate creative ideas and encourage our receptivity to information beyond the domain of the Limited Self. When we visualize and affirm positive suggestions as we fall asleep, we deepen our access to the unconscious, the

God-stream of knowing. Thus we can speed up and strengthen our results.

Using Pre-sleep Suggestions to Clarify Our Higher Life Purpose

The border between waking and sleep is a powerful state. The following affirmation can be helpful in tapping its potential:

I give thanks, for in the sleeping state, clarity comes to me regarding my higher life purpose, and the greatest positive use of my life energy.

The difficulty for so many of us is that we have never fully explored what is our "life" work. Jobs may provide "vehicles" for earning necessary income for our independence and the meeting of our obligations. But do we feel that the job is congruent with our life purpose? How should we best place our energy? A higher life purpose must be in alignment with the soul's nature and the best use of our time, energy, resources, and possibilities.

Are our current roles carved out by default? Have we been attempting to live someone else's dream for us? Although we have an obligation to our present circumstances, it does not mean that we have lost the right to explore other avenues of meaningful, creative participation in life. Don't we desire a life of greater peace, joy, and happiness? That possibility begins with permission to explore, imagine, and create. That exploration does not make us exempt from duty, responsibility, and rightful attention to those who are dependent upon us in our family. Despite such prescribed roles, we should not see ourselves as limited in our capacity to explore our creative experience.

As we enter the pre-sleep state, the ego-based consciousness is less active and less vigilant. This is an advantage because the Limited Self does not like to receive messages that lessen its own role. Whatever our preconceptions around self-identity, they are powerfully guarded and influenced by the ego. It readily goes into assault, or defensive modes of resistance, when preconceptions are challenged by different ideas.

On the other hand, the Eternal Self has no need to defend. There is expansiveness in truth and in the vibration of love. The Eternal Self has no preconceptions. It simply is in a state of perfect Being. Suggestions that resonate with the truth of the soul will be acted upon. Our intention and alignment with truth facilitates an inevitable response.

Any suggestion in the pre-sleep state will act as a stimulus for the direct participation of the Eternal Self. An affirmation which states, "When I sleep, I create" gives permission and direction to the subconscious to bring into our experience our most desired goals and needs. The greater the alignment and attunement between the Limited Self and the Eternal Self, the greater will be the possibility of bridging impermanent states of happiness to enduring states of joy.

To utilize the technique of auto-suggestion (self-suggestion), follow these simple steps:

- Envision white light around you and give thanks that you are divinely protected and divinely inspired by the power and the force of the universe, or God. (Petition a power higher than yourself in whatever manner makes you comfortable.)
- After you have mentally surrounded yourself with white light, state that ideas of inspiration and creativity are now manifesting. Possible affirmations that could be used are:

> *"My mind incubates the creative flow."*
>
> *"My mind is inspired with creative solutions."*
>
> *"I am inspired by powerful, creative solutions in my career life and in my personal life."*
>
> *"Spirit inspires solutions that come to me with clarity while in the dreaming and sleeping state."*
>
> *"I am creative mind. I am inventive mind. I access knowing."*
>
> *"I penetrate truth. I am inspired by the Infinite Thought."*

While in this pre-sleep state, continue to repeat any of these sentences, or other similar ideas, while focusing your energy on the screen of your forehead, at the point between the eyebrows ("spiritual eye"). Proceed with intention and receptivity, as if it is inevitable that you will receive a divine positive response. Your consciousness should not be entertaining doubts about your capacity to receive or create.

Keep a notebook, or paper and pencil, near your bedside to assist you in recording thoughts, ideas, or inspirations that may come to you in that resting (pre-sleep) or sleeping state. Develop the habit of writing down these thoughts, as it will encourage your focus of intention and your ability to be a receiver of inspiration. Thoughts not written down or recorded may rapidly disappear. If you continue with this practice night after night, you will find that sleep incubates creative thought.

You can also do affirmations around specific creative areas, such as music, writing, and art. After you have mentally placed the white light of protection around yourself, then mentally repeat, "I am inspired in my music, art, writing, etc. The power of inspiration and creativity are manifesting in magnificent form now."

Another affirmation:

> *"As I sleep, I create.*
> *As I sleep, I invent.*
> *As I sleep, I solve all problems."*

Time Management

The subject of time management may appear to be in direct opposition to the concept of creative flow. Many feel that creative flow moves with the greatest force if unhampered by human constraints. But even the most powerful river is contained on either side as it moves toward the ocean. "Containing" (managing) our time is essential if our creative flow is to move toward its fullest, most oceanic expression. Providing the proper time and place for our creativity is necessary, just as it is for any worthy endeavor.

A tempting way of avoiding our fears regarding creativity is to hide our potential under the excuse of having no time. We must build in some structured time to exercise our creativity if it is to expand.

In reality, the more we are centered and aligned with our self, the greater our access to inspiration, and the more connected we are to the stream of all creation. The more fragmented we are, the less consistent is our access. We can train our consciousness to become more imaginative by exercising imagination. Consciousness is pliable and can be trained to develop wonderful habits of creativity.

The habit that we are attempting to cultivate, above all, is discipline. Discipline is directly tied to will-based activity. Will-based intention is consistently moved forward by discipline. Discipline strengthens will. Through discipline we can train the consciousness to increasingly expand in imagination and visualization. When we set aside time just to imagine success in creative endeavors and to practice the habit of gratitude, we will reinforce both the spiritual quality of gratitude and the habit of creativity through a greater alignment with the Creator.

How many great talents and creative endeavors die because of the lack of discipline? We have all experienced the desire to learn something new -- to paint, or to take up a musical instrument, or write our memoirs, for example. Procrastination sets in. Before we know it, another year, or two, has gone by. There is no time like the present to begin. This requires discipline. Through discipline we learn to persevere. As Thomas Edison is reputed to have said, "All great ideas involve 10% inspiration and 90% perspiration." Time management is critical to the cultivation of discipline and, hence, to a heightened expression of our creativity.

Discipline is vital to any worthy endeavor, such as losing weight, eating healthier, exercising more, or learning a new skill. It is especially important in a spiritual practice such as meditation, which is an essential component to a happy creative life. Meditation is so much more than a way of relaxing and entering into a heightened state of peace. To view it as such will certainly bring benefits, but only minimal success. Having a meditation practice that is balanced and systematic helps develop an interiorized state of knowing. Peace does not just happen by chance, nor does accessing creativity. It is the cultivated outcome of a disciplined practice. The more we meditate with keen attention, the more consistently we are able to access deeper states of consciousness. And the deeper we go into consciousness, the more our creative channel opens. By adding meditation to our daily routine, we dramatically enhance the progress of our creative journey.

How to be More Effective in Utilizing Time Management:

- Analyze how we use our time: Is time managing us, or are we managing time? Write down how our time is spent on a daily basis, analyzing our overall patterns.
    a. Work activities.
    b. Recreational activities.
    c. Casual conversation on the telephone.
    d. Non-work activities: reading, the Internet, television, etc.
- Be sure to include some creative activities each day. This "appointment" with ourselves should be seen as a gift -- a time of play and reconnection with our spirit and essence.
- Set small goals at first. Giving ourselves small periods of time to work on specific projects can be a way of increasing skill and refining the use of time. Even if it is 15-30 minutes a day, develop the habit of building creativity into the schedule.
- Schedule quality time. Spend at least 15-30 minutes a day imagining yourself as creative, happy, grateful for your creative nature. This will awaken both imagination and gratitude.
- Keep a Journal. Writing about our dreams and goals makes them more real and signals to the subconscious mind that we are serious about change. The process of writing creates greater commitment. We should be sure to include any non-practical ideas and goals. That is, do not omit things that we feel have no possibility of fruition. The attitude of judging hope, imagination, and creativity

as non-practical stifles both inspiration and imagination. Include practical steps to explore creative interests.
- Prioritize Activities. We always find the time to do the things that are important to us. If we have time to sit and read a newspaper, a magazine, or watch a television show, we have some time available to devote to creative projects.
- Restore necessary balance. Remember that extremes in activity levels do not necessarily rebalance the scales. A balanced life restores our energy and allows for even more inspiration. Excessive work results in imbalance. If we have a demanding work schedule, there may be times when we want to relax or unwind after the "busy-ness" of activities. This is necessary. Too often, however, we may go from excessive activity to excessive loafing.

We have all heard the term "workaholic." Do we have these tendencies? If so, are we fully aware of the consequences to our lives and to our happiness? Excessive preoccupation with work, without inner exploration of one's self, and failure to prioritize meaningful relationships, will produce one-sidedness and lack of harmony.

We more easily become attached to our roles when we identify with the Limited Self, which has no sense of self beyond the parameters of worldly, role-related activities. This is how the small self perceives, measures and presents itself, while the Eternal Self is pure being, pure consciousness, unallied to roles. When locked into the smallness of the Limited Self, our awareness also becomes narrower. Embarking on the journey of discovering ourselves as creative beings is a vital and important step towards further alignment between the two selves and tapping into the creative aspect of all life and all creation.

Journaling as a Creative Tool

Journaling is the technique of writing down our thoughts and feelings without censoring our ideas. It involves allowing free-flowing thoughts, emotions and ideas to be what they are, unhindered. Ideas, thoughts, and grammar need not be edited with a reader in mind. Such writing provides clarity about ourselves and leads to meaningful self-dialogue.

Keeping a journal handy makes it easier to develop the habit of writing down our thoughts upon awakening or retiring. It is important to have a time for self-reflection at least twice a day for 15-20 minutes. It is in this free-flow writing process that the flow of consciousness becomes more transparent. Journaling is a wonderful tool of self-discovery and can increase our communication with ourselves.

Journaling also allows us to experiment with imagination and dreams: the dreams we live in the present and the dreams we long to express. Journaling provides another level of communication between the conscious mind and the unconscious mind and can increase alignment of the Limited Self and the Eternal Self.

Journaling may also be used to clarify goals and map out the ways to achieve them. To be successful, you begin by identifying and setting small, attainable goals with a projected timeline that is realistic. Then give yourself permission just to begin. For instance, if you are interested in art, scheduling a time for yourself to walk around an art store is an excellent beginning. Another goal could be that you ask for information on a good book for a beginner. You may want to pursue information on classes or books and material available in an area that you have previously enjoyed. Develop strategies which make it feel more real to investigate areas of interest.

Some questions to explore when journaling:

a. List three areas of artistic or creative expression that you have wanted to try, expand, or revisit from the past.

b. When considering new or past areas of creativity or interest, what anxieties or fears come up? Do you fear failure? Or do you have fears about what would happen if you did succeed?

c. Is the thought of significant change frightening? Why? Does the idea of significant change interfere with any part of your present self-image? How does the idea of significant change impact your deservedness issues?

d. Are you able to give yourself permission to play with your creativity? Or are you fixated on the final outcome of your creative expression? (Being impatient or uncomfortable with the creative process could undermine your journey. Relaxing and playing with creativity allows you to explore. It is good to focus on process rather than outcome.)

e. Have you had an idea, plan, or concept that you felt may have some value in practical application? Do you credit yourself as being someone who has creative ideas?

f. Do you have the idea for an invention, or a modification of something that has already been marketed? Do you feel it might be worth pursuing any creative or inventive ideas?

g. List three areas that you would like to express more creativity in the *practical* areas of your life, i.e., career, projects such as reorganizing the home or office, or simply using creative modification as a problem-solving tool.
h. Identify some ways of approaching creative interests that you feel would give you greater permission to explore. How can you better give yourself permission just to begin?

Becoming More Self-Aware

Journaling enhances introspection and improves self-dialogue. We cannot change what we do not know. Journaling will allow us to visit our fears—both those that are known to us and those that lie deeper, buried in our unconscious. Writing can clarify areas of emotional difficulty and undo blockages, thus giving us a greater feeling of control over our lives.

We cannot underestimate the power of self-knowledge. We cannot uproot tenacious fear energy without first identifying it. As Socrates wrote, "The unexamined life is not worth living." By bringing in the light of understanding, the "darkness" of our fears becomes illumined. Only then can we release them.

If we feel that we should not explore our creativity, is the reason for this fear-based? If so, the first step in overcoming this fear is becoming aware of its influence in our lives. Fear related to our creative energy may simply be due to the habit of self-negation or feelings of lack of deservedness and worthiness. We can, at last, look at this tendency through the new lens of understanding. This broader perspective allows us to confront those issues more clearly, identifying their root cause and eliminating them from our lives. Keep in mind that habit patterns in consciousness may become our destiny. Every effort to bring them to light and to eradicate those that do not serve us, is one step further toward freedom and creative self-expression. Consciousness, energy and manifestation are intrinsically linked.

By the use of imagination, self-permission to change, renewed intention and inspiration we create a new destiny. The re-awakening of creativity presents keys that will open new doors of self-esteem and self-valuing. We gain more access to the truth of our own nature by the alignment of the Limited and Eternal Selves. With that increased merging, we tap into the dynamo of powerful creation itself. As we become more aware of the Creator within, we experience the Creator without, for we are connected with the power of all creation.

Obstacles to Claiming Our Creative Self

If we look closely within, we will see that there are two main obstacles to accessing our creative self: the fear of failure and the fear of success. Behind most creative blocks is either one or the other. Many times one of these fears will manifest in the form of a paralyzing creative block that does not allow us to produce or follow-through. Sometimes we choose to do nothing rather than risk failure or success; this is a defensive strategy that protects the self from others' judgments, assessments, and criticisms of our inadequacy. How we choose to participate in our own creativity reflects how our consciousness has framed its expectations around deservedness or worthiness. Fear proceeds from deep in the unconscious. We may be unaware of its cause.

This is why journaling is vital. It is essential that we uproot the causes of constrictions that prevent us from exploring our creative nature.

Fear of Failure

We pay a heavy price for our fear of failure. It is a powerful obstacle to growth. It assures the progressive narrowing of the personality and prevents exploration and experimentation. There is no learning without some difficulty and fumbling.
John W. Gardner, novelist

Fear of failure is something most of us, at some time or another, have experienced. This is especially true when it comes to our own creativity, for creativity involves exposing deeper parts of ourselves.

As with the fear of success, the fear of failure can involve some level of psychological projection. What exactly is psychological projection? In Freudian psychology, *psychological projection* or *projection bias* is referred to as a defense mechanism. Projection involves unconsciously denying one's own attributes, thoughts, and emotions, and instead attributing those to the outside world or to other people who are imagined or *projected* to have those feelings.

Said in another way, all that we perceive outside the self is a mirror of something within us. Everything that we see outside is a 'projection'. We project our energy, both positive and negative, onto other people and assume it is within them, often denying that it is within us. When we feel unworthy, at fault, or inadequate, we may keep those feelings unconscious, redirecting (or "projecting") them onto another.

Projection relates to our fears around creativity if we are not aware of our own internal dynamics and assumptions. We can easily mislead ourselves into thinking that there is "truth" in our lack of creative ability. We assume that others do not find us capable, talented, having potential or worthy of success. This type of projection, which is not an accurate assessment of ourselves, can keep us locked in faulty self-definition.

Furthermore, if we received no validation or encouragement of our creative efforts as children, we may go through life without a solid sense of self, afraid to take risks in the domain of creative expression. We lack confidence. Having low self-esteem, we may project that others, too, have no faith in our abilities. This can turn into a self-fulfilling prophecy: we unconsciously create situations in which people do not support us so that we "validate" these feelings of unworthiness.

Early experiences of shame, embarrassment, and unworthiness, may re-emerge throughout our lives, triggered by events, relationships, or the inner movement of consciousness as unresolved issues surface. Fears of being exposed as "untalented" arise. Projection then validates our own faulty self-perception.

Such themes of worthiness and deservedness can subtly adopt various forms that show up as obstacles. Assessing our own worth by the perceived opinions of others leaves us vulnerable and stuck in a cycle of helplessness. For many, the fear of failure thwarts, or permanently halts even minimal efforts at expressing their own creativity.

In All Thy Getting, Get Understanding (Prov. 4:7)

The good news is that our awareness of these principles alone can be liberating. Awareness marks the birth of understanding. Journaling, along with the other practices described in this book, gives us the power to stand firm in the face of fear and not be overwhelmed by it or succumb to a distorted perception of the self.

Part of the remedy when confronting our fear of failure is the practice of self-dialogue and self-exploration. We have to remain ever mindful of the negative self-talk that echoes as loud chatter, berating and diminishing our own capabilities. Conscious attention to self-dialogue combined with journaling to clarify mental processes help expand the creative drive. Such practices also dissolve the shadows we cast upon our own creative process.

Our ultimate goal is to gain greater alignment and integration with the Limited Self and the Eternal Self. The more we do this, the more our negative self talk will cease, and the less power the negativity of others will have over us. We will dramatically decrease our own struggles with worthiness and deservedness as we shift our identity to a much larger and more accurate assessment of ourselves.

Regardless of our fears and struggles, change is always possible. Each effort we make on the path of life strengthens our confidence and our self knowing. If we have a solid enough sense of self, the opinions of others will not be enough to deter us from our creative endeavors. Failures will not devastate us. They may discourage us, surely, and we may be hurt by them, but we do not internalize them so deeply that they become our reality. Our natural urge to express, our innate curiosity about life propels us forward despite any lack of positive reinforcement. If we believe that we deserve good things, we will take the risk to express our creative nature.

Often the desire for public attention and fame around creative efforts is an expression of the desire for love and approval that was not experienced in childhood. With sufficient admiration, we may assume that we can capture that love. But without self-validation and feelings of self-love, no audience would be sufficiently large enough to fill the internal void. Developing the art of contentment within the self, and giving ourselves permission to learn, explore and try new things without external approval are necessary to release the fear of failure.

Fear of Success

We can all relate to the fear of failure, but perhaps not so readily to the fear of success. If we take a deeper look at this fear, however, perhaps it, too, has had an influence in our lives.

For example, have we ever felt timid about exposing our talents, our deeper selves, to others? Have we ever entertained the thought that being successful might represent change, and that change might be uncomfortable, even dangerous? Would we open ourselves more to others' criticism, rejection or ridicule? Perhaps an underlying fear is that we are not worthy of success. If that fear exists, even unconsciously, we may feel safer remaining where we are and not trying something new. Such thoughts and feelings may lie just beneath the surface of our awareness, influencing or even thwarting our efforts to move forward.

The core thought of being unworthy of success has enormous power. It may hide unrecognized behind thoughts such as: "Your success is a fluke. You will never be able to repeat this success or be applauded for your creativity again." Or, "You know, you don't deserve the recognition. In the end, people will discover you are a fraud."

If we believe that success is a good thing, on the other hand, and that it won't hurt us or alienate us from others, that we are, deep down, deserving of all good, we won't be afraid or blocked.

Shifting the Cycle of Negativity

Ideas of unworthiness, feelings of inadequacy, and negative self-talk, underlie both fears of failure and success. Such negatives become powerful walls that stifle and curtail the creativity within. From this day forward, let us affirm our creative nature. As we do, we will begin to pull down those walls.

Strategies to confront fear of failure/success:
- Increase positive self-dialogue and self-analysis.
- Analyze habit patterns of consciousness: As we think, so we create.
- Journal about fears related to both success and failure.
- Be willing to be a beginner.
- Focus on the journey; avoid preoccupation with the outcome.
- Affirm the creative power within; intend to explore and expand it.
- Experiment with, or learn, new areas of interest.
- Schedule time for creativity.

- Exercise imagination by allowing creative inspiration to flow.
- Give thanks in affirmations for the unfolding of divine creativity.
- Practice meditation. Emphasize Aum technique of Self-Realization Fellowship (available through a home-study course online at http://www.yogananda-srf.org/).
- Visualize being involved in successful, creative endeavors.
- Mentally give thanks for this creative aspect of life.
- Be creative in problem-solving and using inventive consciousness.
- Utilize positive visualizations as well as affirmations.
- Practice affirmations on creativity and worthiness to confront deservedness issues and invite the expansion of your creativity.

Creativity begins with small steps that are within reach. If you have always wanted to paint, for example, learn some basics in drawing or sketching. Try to learn the principles involved in depicting light, shadow and perspective from a book or a class. (An excellent book on art is *Drawing from the Right Side of Your Brain,* by Betty Edwards.) Or if you've always wanted to play or write music, be willing to learn. Visualize yourself doing creative activities, relaxed and successful.

Be willing to be a beginner! So many people lament that they are not masters of a particular artistic form. But all true masters in any field started as beginners. There is no shame in having no previous experience. There is, however, great sadness in not giving ourselves permission to try.

Throughout this book you will notice references to the importance of giving ourselves permission to change. Underneath this permission is the faith that we *can* change and that the

Universe will *support* us when we try. Once given, that permission will open creativity to us in ways that are boundless and limitless. It will move our life and our energy with inspiration and imagination along new lines of creativity.

Finding Our Creative Pulse – A Visualization

Begin by breathing deeply. Deep breathing relaxes the mind and body and provides more oxygen to the brain for clearer thought and higher creativity. Always come back to your breathing. Is it shallow, or are you breathing freely? Ask yourself: "What would I *really love* to do?" or "What have I been longing to do -- for years?" *Dare* to imagine your new possibilities. Your passion is a guiding light - showing you bright new possibilities in your personal and professional life.

Imagine yourself being given one wish that is guaranteed to come true. If you could do anything in the world, and if success were assured, what would you do? Let your consciousness roam in the limitless sea of possibilities. Follow the impulses of your heart and soul. Would you be a dancer? A pianist? A clothing designer? An inventor? Allow your imagination to explore the things you have always felt drawn to – your favorite colors, for example, or a beautiful garden setting. Be free to connect with whatever it is that most inspires your passion and interest.

During this exercise, note any images you project onto the movie screen of your imagination; focus at the point between the eyebrows as if it were that screen. Begin the art of imagining and casting your desires into light forms of possibility. Focusing your attention with intention stirs will energy. Dynamic will energizes the scenes you imagined.

Once your desires begin to manifest, make certain that they are aligned with spiritual principle. To gratify the self at the expense or detriment of others is not aligned with spiritual principle. Others have a right to their wants, needs, and desires. When you project your dreams, be certain that they will not be harmful, even unintentionally, to others.

Remember, the Limited Self can create energized attachment to the ideas and scenes it visualizes, so discernment is required. Attachment to our desires also sends the Limited Self into a flurry of activity which intensifies desires, actions, and activities grounded in ego-based consciousness. This, then, diminishes our awareness of the Eternal Self. The desired objects, or experiences, become identified in our mind as being the source of our happiness. As this occurs, we lessen our own inclination to focus on greater integration with the Eternal Self.

The Joy is in the Journey

The joy is in the journey, not the destination. Happiness comes from reaching out to our dreams, tapping into our deepest hearts and allowing life to fully express itself. If we believe that joy will only come to us because we have achieved a final destination, we will have minimized the journey. And it is in the journey that we expend our life energy and creativity and become a new force of creation. Joy results from attending to our consciousness at this moment in time. If we focus sufficient attention on attending to our consciousness, we will penetrate the outer fabric of life into the innermost domain of Being. In doing so, we touch the Eternal Now and our nature is transformed.

Becoming preoccupied with the end product of the creative adventure robs us of pleasure in that process and can intensify fear of failure or success in the pursuit of creative endeavors.

See your efforts as a gift of your time and energy to the universe. As Lord Krishna counsels in the *Bhagavad Gita*, "Do not attach to the results." When you become preoccupied with the end result, the self-critical voice constricts creative flow. Say mentally or out loud:

"I give this gift of my time, my energy and effort to the universe.
I am aligned with my creative force and power.
The power of creative energy is flowing
and expressing through me."

By placing our consciousness in the present moment, we align the Limited Self with the Eternal Self. The Limited Self darts between time sequences, as well as past and future events. Seldom, if ever, does the ego-driven, Limited Self, experience stillness in the now. Creativity is born in those moments of the now, not in the past and or the future.

When we are absorbed in creative effort, the world stops. We are, for those moments, outside of time, living in the Eternal Now. The act of creation stops the push and pull of polarity and we experience the vastness of our creative self. We experience the stirring of Spirit. The two selves align more closely. And in that greater alignment we draw closer to the face of God and the mirror-reflection of our own divine nature.

Conclusion

We possess within our true nature a dynamo of creative force that desires expression. That force wishes to be a co-participant with the divine Creator. When each of us was created, our consciousness was imbued with the principle of creativity. The very atoms of light danced into form. We are the power of that dream of Spirit. The stirring of imagination and the power of thought energized into form underlies the very expression of our being and our creativity in motion.

We came into being by divine intention and the stirring of possibility. We too have the ability to stir creation into magnificent forms and dynamic images of infinite and varied possibilities. Be willing to dream your dreams. Blow breath into your dreams. Give your imagination the power of movement. Movement finds its force by intention that is arrow-driven by dynamic will.

Creation flows from our use of dynamic will, an electrified force field shimmering with every dream that could ever be entertained. Celebrate the inexhaustible possibilities! Go beyond any limiting ideas that diminish your life or the lives of others. We must affirm our truth in order to claim our energy. The absolute power of creation resides within us. Tapping into and dynamically expressing that creative force is our birthright.

We were born out of the vision of God. The Creator of all instilled within us the power of creativity. The keys to the universe were placed in our hands and our right to the throne of creation was given to us as heir apparent. To bemoan our lack of talent or vision and our power as a creator is to denounce creation itself. Universes of possibilities move within us just as the heavenly bodies rotate in divine perfection in deep space. Let us capture the heavenly energy within and give it form.

True humility means to claim our oneness as a spark of that great overarching Spirit that is within all things. To deny our Source or our abilities is neither humility nor accuracy of perception. The divine force of the universe has created us so that one day we will confidently claim our truth by penetrating into our light nature. We will feel the power within us moving in joyous expression of self-knowing. All empowerment expresses true self-claiming. We will know ourselves as Spirit moving in creation, unbounded by the flesh and the limitations of the world. We will know ourselves as awake and alive in the Eternal Present! Our inspiration, imagination and our flight with Spirit gives us universes to travel, wings to fly, and solar systems to explore.

Penetrate into the Stillness: A Note on Meditation

If the doors of perception were cleansed, everything would appear to us as it is, Infinite.

--William Blake

All beings, no matter how reactive, fearful, violent or lost, can open themselves to the sacred within and become free. Spirit is our very being. Meditation allows us access to the deeper regions of our spiritual nature, connects us with the Divine presence within, and provides us a clearer vision of the truth. Scheduling time each day for meditation practice is essential not only for peace and well-being, but for experiencing our Eternal Selves, the true source of lasting happiness. Countless meditation techniques are available. Finding an effective and suitable style of meditation can take time and experimentation but will prove invaluable. One technique is offered below.

Begin with the proper posture for meditation:

- Sitting in a straight back chair is recommended.

- The feet should be flat on the floor, pointed straight ahead.

- In a state of relaxation, maintain a straight spine, to the best of your ability without straining or discomfort.

- Place your hands, with palms turned gently upward, near the junction between your hips and legs or lower down on your thighs. Note: Meditation techniques, in general, should not be practiced in a position where the individual is lying down in a bed. When lying down, the meditative state too easily becomes a sleep state. If an individual has the physical ability to sit either in a chair with feet flat on the floor—or cross-legged on the floor on a flat surface, the sitting posture should be assumed. In general avoid sitting on a bed, for consciousness usually associates the bed with sleep.

This meditation technique involves focusing your attention at the point between the eyebrows known as the "spiritual eye." This is a center that increases our spiritual connectedness as we focus upon it. The following suggestion may assist you in getting the correct angle for your focus gaze. The eyes should be turned gently and slightly upward.

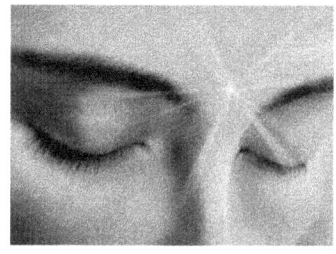

Pencil Technique for Proper Gaze

Visualize holding a #2 pencil eraser at the spiritual eye. (See diagram at left.) Visualize the eraser resting on the forehead between and slightly above the eyebrows, centered at the spiritual eye, with the pencil parallel to the ground. Allow your focus to move to where you visualize the point of the pencil to be. Keep the gaze focused at that spot. This technique is not part of the practice itself, but will prevent you from placing excessive strain on the eyes and help develop a better habit pattern for meditation.

Note: There should be no strain or tension. This is a natural, pleasant position for the eyes.

Preparation for Meditation:

- Visualize that you are encircled by white light which either outlines the body or is shaped as a spherical egg-shape. Mentally placing white light around the body summons a greater connection with Spirit and strengthens the energy field.

- After visualizing the white light in this way, begin to observe the breath in a relaxed state of mind. Maintain the correct posture with spine erect and feet flat on the floor.

- Affirm that you are divinely protected.

Note: Effective meditation techniques are available from the Self-Realization Fellowship in the form of lessons that are delivered to your home every two weeks. For information contact:

Self Realization Fellowship
3880 San Rafael Drive
Los Angeles, CA 900653210
323-225-2471
http//www.yogananda-srf.org

Additional affirmations that may be mentally repeated prior to or after using this meditation technique:

I ride the inward breath.
I ride the outward breath.
I am one with that breath.
Reveal Thyself.

Meditation and affirmations, such as those below, are two of the most powerful spiritual tools. Properly practiced they can release fear related to your divinely-given creativity and help erase deservedness issues that block you. Deservedness is the subject of our next chapter.

Affirmations for Creativity

For Creative Sleep
As I sleep, I create.
As I sleep, I invent.
As I sleep, I solve all problems.

For Full Creativity
By the law of creation,
I am creating.
Spirit is dancing through me.

For Divinely Expanding Creativity
The creative force within me
is the divine energy of God
ever expanding,
ever creating,
ever renewing itself.

For Invoking Imagination
I am Imagination.
Creator within,
pour forth the streams
of imaginative vision.
Unlock my power.
I am imagination -
particles of possibilities
dancing in the light.

For Specific Forms of Creativity
The Divine is expressing itself
through creative expression
in the area of _____.
(fill in with an area of creativity that you desire to increase.)

<u>For Divine Artistry</u>
The Divine
is the artist within me.
I am the art
of the Artist
ever manifesting.

<u>For Dynamic Co-creating</u>
I am an instrument
of divine creativity.
I am a dynamic co-creator
with the universe.
Expansive, creative energy
is manifesting from me NOW.

Chapter Two

Deservedness and How to Feel It

You are invited to the inner journey that affirms your worthiness, deservedness and entitlement to receive the gifts and grace of your potent divine nature.

Our feelings of self-worth and deservedness create or block the flow and manifestation of circumstances in our lives. If we will change our circumstances, we must change our consciousness.

Key topics addressed in this chapter:

- Exploring our beliefs about our deservedness.
- Consciousness creates our circumstances.
- Assessing beliefs about your worthiness/deservedness in receiving.
- Analyzing our own self-dialogue.
- Affirming negative and positive statements.
- Origins of our sense of unworthiness.
- Steps in changing our self-concept.
- Methods of transforming negative self-talk: imagination, dynamic intention, and dynamic, will-charged affirmations.

- Helping to reclaim a sense of deservedness and entitlement.
- The struggle of the Limited Self.
- The power to limit or create via circular energy patterns.
- Shame, guilt, and the role of conscience.
- Inherent Spiritual Truth versus Indoctrination.
- Redemption from shame and guilt by the law of Grace.
- Why we are deserving and entitled.

Self-Exploration of Deservedness

The previous chapter on Creativity has shown that often the greatest obstacle to your full, oceanic expression of creativity can be your own sense of self-worth, or deservedness. In order to remove such obstacles, you must first explore your feelings about your right, entitlement, deservedness, and worthiness to be a receiver of the good in your own life. As a child of God or a divine participant in the universe, do you feel you deserve at a deep core level to be happy, to receive the good including abundance and prosperity? Do you feel you are deserving but for some unknown reason you never had a chance to express your joyous participation in the bounty of life, in the flow of love, in prosperity and happiness? Do you feel life passes you by, no matter how hard you try? Do you perceive your difficulties as coming from bad luck, or do you think that some of your difficulties result from your own habit patterns and repetitive thoughts? Do you feel others are luckier or more entitled to be happy, prosperous, and nurtured than you are?

Our feelings around worthiness and deservedness are powerful factors influencing not only our role as a generator of possibilities, but also in shaping our relationship with the Divine. Our struggles with feeling the right to have a meaningful relationship with Spirit is partly determined by our feelings of worthiness in general.

The science of psychology offers one valid perspective on happiness and self-esteem. Yet it is man's metaphysical dilemma that frequently hammers the core feeling about our right and our worthiness to receive that greater good. Issues surrounding our perception of being good enough influence how we relate to God or the Divine. Our own ideas of deservedness and our own self-definition dramatically thwart or support our pursuit of abundance, prosperity and ultimately, happiness.

As we believe we deserve, we fuel and project deeper feelings and patterns of emotions. If there exist deep feelings that we are undeserving of receiving the good, that concept may undermine our sincere and genuine efforts at change, including spiritual efforts and techniques. We must get clear about the attitudes and habits of consciousness within us. The greater our feelings of unworthiness and lack of deservedness, the greater will be the resistance to systematically using techniques of change, including visualization, affirmation, and meditation. If we are to counter negative ideas, we must become more aware of our habitual thought patterns. We must substitute negative, repetitive thoughts with positive, affirming affirmations.

Feelings of unworthiness always translate into some type of negative self-statement. This negative self-statement becomes a negative affirmation. These negative ideas become projected themes around our self-identification. Any energized theme that directly, or indirectly, states our lack of entitlement becomes an affirmation. In a sense, the negative thought becomes a mantra of living, an energized thought form operating by the law of magnetism and attraction, like bringing forth like.

Such negative affirmations may be counteracted by the use of powerful positive affirmations proclaimed with dynamic intention of will.

Journey in Consciousness Exploration

We all have the power to negate ourselves as a creator and as a potent life and light force in the universe. We also all have the power to begin to create a new reality consistent with the innate harmony within ourselves, with others, with nature, and with Spirit. Shifting our consciousness from a role as victim to one as divine co-creator can unleash our own power to create the positive instead.

Do you see yourself as a creator? As a victim trapped by the past? Do you believe you have the ability to change? Do you believe you have the power to pursue a journey that will lead to a transformation of consciousness? The answers to these questions are pivotal.

Introspection Opportunity

What are the areas of your life that you would like to change?
- What are the areas in which you could experience greater success, reward, or happiness by increasing positive flow?
- List the areas in which you desire to see dramatic change, knowing change cannot occur without rooting up feelings of unworthiness.

Self-Assessment

- How do you assess your self-worth?
- Do you base your assessment on your possessions or status in the material world?
- Do you assess your worth based on meaningful relationships or deep moments of connection with others?
- Do you define your worth on the capacity to receive or to give? Or a combination of these attributes?
- Do you assess your worth and define who you are based on your personality traits and feedback from others?
- Or do you possess a deep place of self-knowing independent from societal values, impressions of others, or definitions of the world? In that deep place, is there a part of you that feels you are more than you, yourself know? Is that self beyond the access of the perception of others and the definition of the world itself?

The Power of our Self-Assessment

Honest answers to these questions are key to your self-assessment:

- Do you feel entitled to receive, to benefit, and to extract good, abundance, peace, joy, and happiness in your life?
- Do you feel worthy to claim and take that profound journey tied to your innermost essence?
- Are you waiting to feel good enough, perfect enough, lovable enough, creative or talented enough, to claim more of yourself?

Introspection Exercise:

Write five experiences, inspirations or events that have allowed you to progress or succeed in some aspect of your life.

Then write five events, episodes or repeated themes that impacted you, from your early life, in a negative way.

Having a clearer idea of the negative and positive ideas that have impacted your life may help you understand how you repeat themes about yourself in your internal dialogue. It may also give you an understanding of how those positive and negative experiences tend to repeat in the patterns of adult life.

How does your spiritual perception of yourself equate with the way others define who you are? Do you see yourself as disconnected from Spirit, from God, or your own spiritual nature? Do you believe that you have a spiritual nature? In your spiritual assessment of yourself, are you more likely to view yourself as fallen, a sinner? Or do you view yourself as a divine child of God? Do you feel unworthy to be recognized, honored, or part of a Higher Power? Do you have an expansive view of yourself aligned with spiritual truth? Do you engage in negative self-talk? Or do you affirm who you are positively? Do you expect change to happen as instant transformation and instant gratification? Perhaps real change may involve consistency of effort and spiritual principles.

Write down what you feel your circumstances or conditions will be in one year, three years, five years, and ten years. Analyze what things you put on the list. Do you see yourself as initiating and having power over the changes or being a recipient of good fortune and opportunities from others? Or perhaps both?

If you, at a deep level, feel that you are unworthy, or that you do not deserve to be loved, or to be prosperous, successful, or to be spiritual, again you will find those manifestations originated from your thought, the origin of ideas. Neutral thoughts have minimal energy. Energized thought, whether negative or positive, creates your material circumstances. What you say to yourself becomes truth, whether or not it has any basis or substance in fact.

The unconscious mind will not evaluate the truth of a statement; it will operate as if all statements are true. You must be very careful what you say about yourself and what you affirm to be true. For instance, if you have experienced a failure around a particular project or endeavor, do you state the project or endeavor "failed," or do you state, "I am a failure"? Do you see the setback as tied to a particular situation or circumstance, or do you state it in a way that defines you? The repetition of such thoughts as, "I am a failure or, my good ideas never succeed," will continue to create a dynamic flow in direct opposition with that with which you desire. When you personalize negative ideas into statements about yourself, you create negative dialogue and life themes that constrict the flow of positive, dynamic energy. Constricted energy inhibits personal expansion, belief in self, and the ability to access our true powers.

Some self-help books and popular psychologists recommend the use of simple visualization techniques as magical tools for manifesting your deepest desires.

Alluring as these sound in their seeming effortlessness, simple visualization techniques are limited unless accompanied by efforts towards deeper, internalized changes in consciousness. Will-directed intention, projected with affirming truths, on the other hand, can create sustained changes in consciousness, circumstances, and manifestation.

A sense of worthiness, entitlement, and deservedness, must be stated and restated, fortified by the intention of focused will and concentration in order to develop a sufficient force field of the positive. This is necessary to counter negative self-talk. If like is to attract like, we must be generators of the positive and we must be able to state the truth of our rightful role in pursuing, expressing, and possessing happiness, peace, serenity, well-being, and spiritual awareness. You <u>are</u> entitled to happiness! You are entitled to be a receiver of the good! You are a powerful co-creator with the universe, summoning the light of universes!

Introspection Opportunity

Assessing beliefs about your worthiness/deservedness in receiving.

On a scale from 1-5, let 5 indicate strong feelings of worthiness and deservedness, with 1 indicating feelings of unworthiness and lack.

1. Do you feel you are deserving or worthy of being loved? Rate yourself on a scale of 1-5.
2. Do you feel you deserve or are worthy to participate in abundance, prosperity? Rate yourself on a scale of 1-5.
3. In the area of health and wellbeing, do you feel you deserve greater health and wellness? Do you feel you deserve to be ill because of previous health or life choices? Rate those on the scale of 1-5.
4. Do you feel you deserve happiness and success that involves expressing creativity? Do you feel you are

worthy of considering yourself a creative, inspired individual? Also on a scale 1-5.
5. Do you feel you are deserving and entitled to a higher level of relationship with yourself, with the universe, or with God? Do you make statements such as, "I am too unworthy, not good enough, or spiritually undeserving"?

In order to determine whether early issues continue to limit the flow of good in our lives, we must pay close attention to the pattern of negative self-statements that we make in times of stress or crisis. What do we say to ourselves when something negative happens? What is the pattern of those thought processes? Around the area of love, do we have any ideas or statements that we are not truly good enough to be loved? Do you believe that your relationships are doomed to failure or do you resign yourselves to a state of mediocrity? Do you see yourself as a creator with a capacity to create the best in life and possibilities? Do you make statements about your limitations in prospering and in achieving true abundance, prosperity and a greater flow in all areas of life?

Analyzing Our Own Self-Dialogue:
Destroy the Negative, Create the Positive

We must expand our awareness of our thought patterns, analyze repetitive themes of the mind and emotions, listen to and write down the negative self-statements we make. Becoming more familiar with our own patterns of negative self-talk empowers us to make changes. We can become energy magnets by using positive self-talk and visualizing positive circumstances. If we perceive those events as external and independent from the movement of our consciousness, the less we will make consistent efforts at personal change and consciousness analysis.

Replaying and analyzing our thought patterns throughout the day will give us a clearer indication of how much time we are focused on negative self-themes or positive affirming self-statements.

Write down those themes; give an estimate of the mental time spent around negative self-ideas and around positive self-ideas. Our self-dialogue is powerful because we are supplying, in those ideas, the very energy of creation to begin a true process of materialization and manifestation. The power of the Creator is resident within us. The powerhouse of the universe resides within you. Our beings are charged with a thousand suns of possibilities and our minds are the clay-molder of present and future materialization and manifestation in our lives. We have the power! What ideas are revolving in our consciousness as we use this powerful mind source in the act of creation?

You Are Entitled to Change and to Receive

Our deepest fear is not that we are inadequate. Our deepest fear is that we are powerful beyond measure. It is our light, not our darkness that most frightens us. We ask ourselves, Who am I to be brilliant, gorgeous, talented? Actually who are you not to be? You are a child of God. Your playing small does not serve the world...We were born to make manifest the glory of God that is within us, not just in some of us, but in everyone.
--Marianne Williamson

- **Analyze and identify your mental habits** and thought processes to identify those patterns that need to be changed.
- **Internalize the truth** that mental repetition of ideas does not equate with truth or validity.

- **Use will-based intention** in order for change to occur.
- **Increase the positive thoughts** and statements about life, others, and ourselves by identifying those mental habit patterns.
- **Strengthen the habit pattern of more positive thoughts**.
- **Decrease negative thoughts** and statements about life, others, and ourselves by identifying those mental habit patterns.
- **Use spirit-based affirmations systematically** to create vibrational shifts that can truly transform consciousness over time.
- **Proceed with affirmations and positive visualization**, even if you do not believe anything will change.

Know that replacing negative ideas with positive, powerful, spirit-affirming statements can generate positive shifts. These shifts result in the altering of consciousness and the direct manifestation of positive changes in circumstances. These shifts can occur whether or not you believe those thoughts are true, real, believable, or possible.

- Affirm positive change NOW. (Thoughts have the power to blueprint the future and change the NOW.)
- Increase your spiritual participation in life. Pursue that which is deep and meaningful for your life. Be cautious of any organization or group that asks you to transfer your personal power or assets and denies your own capacity to access the highest aspects of yourself or God.

It's important to understand that our deep-seated sense of deservedness or unworthiness has complex origins based on:

- Childhood experiences and interpretations of those experiences.
- Internalized values.
- Circular negative feelings.
- Negative self-talk.
- Shame and guilt.(The shroud of shame dulls the bright light of God within.)

Childhood Experiences

Childhood themes imprint powerfully. In developmental stages throughout childhood we achieve amazing mastery, skill, and abilities as the result of streams of imaginative energy and the power of self-definition. In addition to mastery, competency, and skill sets, we also have internalized negative ideas, messages, and themes. Our imagination not only plays a role in interpreting the events that happen to us, but our imagination projects thoughts about how others see us. Our imagination is the artist's brush by which our self-image is formed. Negative self-talk is a prevalent and destructive result of the improper use of imagination and faulty interpretation of experiences and encounters with others.

Where Did The Negative Self-Talk Begin?

How did the negative themes develop?

1. Negative experiences may occur at early, impressionable ages.

2. Opinions or behaviors may come from our parents, or significant others, in our childhood. (The events that actually occurred.)
3. Perceptions about what occurred; these perceptions can include real and imagined impressions of childhood messages.
4. Repetition of ideas about these experiences and perceptions which expand internalized impressions and messages into persistent self-negating themes for the adult. Ideas become themes.
5. Our continuing self-assessment, self-measurement, and self-talk reinforces these self-negating themes. We tend to replay circular themes based on our earlier imaginative, interpretive experiences.
6. Negatively-interpreted experiences from school or community.
7. Childhood trauma related to violations of trust and abuse.
8. Disruption of early developmental stages as the result of emotional or physical neglect, or adult disconnection.
9. Physical or emotional abandonment (for example, death, divorce, or absence of a significant other in the life of a child).

The child may become handicapped, not only by the experiences of childhood, but by the interpretations of the experiences that occurred at impressionable ages. Perceptions then become energized thought forms.

Early social values internalized in childhood are rooted in such experience and interpretations, but are also influenced by the society in which we are born. Socio-economic values and religious and political views have a sociological backdrop. Messages from the family and significant others and the community intermingle with the existing family structure. Ideas, philosophies, and values are absorbed as we become acculturated. Internalized messages become part of our consciousness.

Children may be psychologically harmed in many ways, including abuse, excessive authoritarian control, minimal positive interaction, emotional neglect, inadequate adult role models. The dysfunction of adults may damage children in ways that make them more susceptible to dysfunction in their adulthood, including problems such as substance abuse, mental illness, or impaired capacity to relate to others.

Early experiences, mentally replayed in our mind, can develop into a pattern of negative self-talk. This negative self-talk becomes themes of early self-identity and self-definition that has the power to carry into adulthood. Who are you really? Are you separate from who you believe yourself to be? Or are you defined by the power of repetitive self-definition, including negative self-talk?

Children often feel that they are the reason adults mistreated, neglected, ignored, abandoned, or abused them. They do not understand the adult psyche, their own psyche, or the adult world. They have no capacity to grasp the psychological issues, or family dynamics of the parents, or others, in their lives.

Because of their inability to grasp the larger picture, children always pull the occurrences back to themselves, as if the mistreatment springs in some manner from their own psyche, behavior, or self-concept. This belief that they are to blame for neglect, adult emotional or mental disconnection, death, abandonment, trust violations, and various forms of abuse has no basis in truth. The child believes powerfully that bad things would not have occurred had they been "good enough."

Children, seeing themselves as the source of trouble in the family, begin to create a foundation of self-negation and low self-esteem. Feelings of unworthiness, and deep core feelings of being undeserving, as well as a sense of spiritual dislocation are all part of self-negation.

Continual criticism by parents about the core of the child create great difficulties in developing positive self-worth and self-esteem. By contrast, parental strategies that correct behaviors rather than attack core identity allow a child to change without needing to alter their basic definition of themselves.

Community values and definitions also have a strong impact on children. They see those values as "real," permanent and having absolute authority. No child has the ability to discriminate, reasonably debate or challenge the existing structure of the society in which he has been born. The child is an information gatherer and an absorber of ideas and energies. When parental and community values are in agreement, the value system is even more formidable, seemingly enduring, and limiting to a child in search of self and alternatives. Greater restriction and less tolerance for diversity result when a community operates within a narrow range of ideas and values.

Damage to the evolving psyche of a child may involve feelings of unworthiness tied to insufficient nurturing and loving. What child does not deserve to be loved? Whether or not a child received adequate loving or nurturing is complicated by how the child perceived the experiences. Replaying the perception, and replaying the interpretation of the perception, energizes those memories until they feel like a core truth.

Rarely before adolescence does a child begin to challenge the status quo. But even when that critical capacity develops, there may be no awareness of how deeply internalized themes continue to play the role of an authoritative judge in one's own life. Rebellion, alone, does not break the powerful concepts where one's identity is held in hostage to belief systems, values, and the group consensus of the community. The child, in this community, is also directly experiencing the uniqueness that has to do with his own family of origin and the uniqueness of how he defines himself.

How do people become programmed with the untruth about themselves? Over time we have all internalized feelings of worthiness or unworthiness, deservedness or lack of deservedness, and entitlement or non-entitlement to receive.

Experiences and perceptions become messages which then become internalized beliefs. These may feel like the core of the self, but are merely an overcoat of experiences, perceptions, and interpretations created by a child in the process of development. This overcoat of ideas may be held tightly around the self. However, there is no inherent truth in this created reality.

Other sources of our sense of deservedness are the opinions of others, and internalized feelings about ourselves. The opinions of others or the criticism of ourselves cannot make us feel fully deserving of love, however.

Methods of Transforming Negative Self-Talk

Energy, charged by will and intention, may assist in replacing negative repetition with positive repetition of ideas. These new energy grooves, by increased repetition and fueled with imagination and intention, carry the promise of change, new creation, and new manifestation. Imagination, dynamic intention, and dynamic affirmations practiced and repeated with regularity will help us harness and direct new energies of creation.

Redefining ourselves as creators of new conditions and circumstances and releasing ourselves from the imprisonment of our own ideas and consciousness will allow us to see ourselves as more than trapped victims of the past. True transformation involves the rooting up of powerful, negative energy grooves from the past. Yogis call these patterns in consciousness *samskaras*. If we are to create a new, positive, affirming self-definition, we must eradicate the habit of negative self-talk. Part of the solution to uprooting this powerhouse of negation involves using the same principle of powerful, energized *positive* thought. Thoughts energized with positive affirmations, imagination and creativity, create a powerhouse of new ideas and mental impressions, changing self-definition and remove negative, self-limiting ideas and energy.

Perhaps most destructively, the chatter of negative self-talk blocks the more subtle vibration tied to Spirit, love, and harmony. The love vibration and spiritual light are less accessible the more the consciousness thrusts outward into the realm of activities. So if we lack integrated self-knowledge of the two selves, we block our deepest experience of ourselves. As long as we feel that Spirit is separate from us, we will believe that we cannot access the divine essence.

Without understanding our two selves, Spirit is seen as separate and in that separateness we feel unable to achieve connection or happiness. In order to achieve greater integration and inner peace within the Limited Self, the powerful impediment of feelings of unworthiness and lack of deservedness must be addressed. As we redefine our deservedness, the energy lines of creation and the law of attraction and magnetism will follow. When we disrupt a powerful negative cycle, we free up energy for new creation and new lines of attraction resulting in positive manifestation.

Journal Exercise:
Victim or Creator?

Write in your journal about the following subjects:
- Do you see yourself as the victim of present or past circumstances?
- Do you feel you are trapped in your present circumstances? Or do you feel you are a victim now because of your past?
- Do you see yourself as having the power to create the new and co-create potent new possibilities?
- Do you feel a new surge of power in creating the now and the future? What must occur for you to feel that you deserve more than is your present set of circumstances and conditions?
- Do you feel you are entitled to the good?

- Do you feel worthy to receive more happiness and positive circumstances in your life?

Feelings of unworthiness and feelings that you do not fully deserve the love of others, yourself, or God poison the power that is yours in claiming the fullness of your life. Such negative self-assessment and repetitive self-dialogue can distort the fullness of the experience of being human and the fullness of the experience of being Spirit in human form. To deserve or not to deserve, that is the question. Whether it is nobler to resign yourself to a less deserved state or to risk the power of change embedded within yourself by the power of creation itself!

More on Negative Self-Talk

Ideas do not originate separate from a source. Ideas and thoughts, however, may feel as if they have always been with us. They may feel as if they are intrinsic to our self, yet the truth is they may be alien and foreign to the truth of our nature. They may be distortions that deny the true essence of our nature, our connection to Spirit, and our connection with one another. Thoughts may feel as if they are true simply because we have practiced, over time, repeating them.

Exercise on Negative Self-Talk

1. Write down ten sentences you remember your father saying to you.
2. Then write down ten sentences you remember your mother saying to you.
3. If another caregiver was significant in your early life other than parents, do the exercise for that individual.

Go over those sentences again and examine whether you repeat any of those sentences to yourself, either in crises or on a regular, on-going basis not crisis related. Do the words shape your dialogue with yourself? Or did that impression of yourself develop without input or the use of imagination and interpretation?

Will-charged affirmations and concentrated thought, explicit in visualization, will help you redefine the truth of your existence. Never doubt that the power of creation resides within us. From that source of energy all universes, all forms, have sprung into the vibrational existence of matter. By the repetition of vibrational truth in sound more of the potency of our own nature is unlocked. Using energized repetition in the form of spiritualized affirmation may unlock an unharnessed power that can truly transform consciousness.

Some may link the idea of deservedness directly to how much faith one possesses. Some communities may judge the impulse to inquire, analyze, or question as a threat to faith. They may even equate questioning with alienation from the love of God. If we internalize that value, we dismiss our own critical mind, which has the need and capacity to inquire and understand. In some circles, to ask is to question; to question is to doubt; to doubt is to be unworthy; to be unworthy is to be denied access to God or God's love. The soul nature desires to know and perceive. We need to invite all, young and old, to a journey of positive exploration, supporting their ability to know, to perceive, and transform awareness in affirmative, exalting ways.

Interpretations become energized by circular replay

Feelings of unworthiness create pervasive and persistent attitudes about our right to receive. Feelings become themes. Themes repeat into a circular pattern of energy replay. The repetition deepens the theme. The deepened themes around worthiness attract similar or like energy by the law of attraction and magnetism.

By the acts of mental repetition, and not by truth, thought energy circulates around the themes of entitlement. This energy then attracts the flow of like or similar energy by the law of attraction and magnetism
Mental ideas and thoughts are the images we replay. Mental thoughts replay into themes; the act of circular replay becomes our truth.

The Power to Limit or Create via Circular Energy Patterns

As our thoughts repeat ideas about ourselves and our possibilities, we create circular energy patterns. These circular energy patterns create the energy grooves or *samskaras* that deepen by repetition. Negative circular energy patterns are intensified by the mental cycle of repetitive thought. These thought processes limit new positive inroads of possibilities, and thus limit more positive manifestation.

We become what we claim is our nature. If we make repetitive, negative statements about our tendencies and possibilities, we will find our lives reflect those statements of limitation. Similarly, if we repeat energized, positive statements by harnessing the power of focused will we will find our lives reflect new and different positive possibilities. We become creators of new grooves of energy and new universes of possibilities.

Shame and Guilt

The feelings and emotions associated with guilt and shame may drastically affect our capacity to feel worthy of receiving. Yet our guilt and shame may not reflect any truth about us. These feeling states do reflect our values, our ideas, our perceptions of the right and the wrong in life and in our behaviors. And sometimes these perceptions are an intuitive knowing that spiritual laws have been violated by not honoring life and light. But very often, feelings of shame and guilt result from a restrictive childhood in which shame was a tool of discipline and adults constantly reinforced the negative to a child in the process of learning, growing, and becoming. In that situation, guilt results, though unjustly.

Other clarifications about feelings of guilt and shame:
- If based on accurate assessment of your previous behaviors, deeds, or lack of understandings, then your feelings may be justified.
- If based on accurate assessments and perception, you need to reshape your consciousness and behaviors.

- If based on inaccurate assessments and perception, you need to free yourself from our own power of misunderstanding.
- Reform and reshape these feelings with introspection, self-examination and explorations of consciousness and spirit.

Answers to these questions may also shine valuable light on the issue of conscience:

- Is it our conscience which allows us to feel shame and guilt?
- Does our conscience arise out of the messages of our childhood and environmental experiences? Or does conscience have an origin in a higher, intuitive, deeper place of knowing?
- What are your thoughts about conscience? Do you feel you have an over-developed conscience? Are you excessively hard on yourself over minor infractions which invoke deep, shame-based feelings?
- Do you find it difficult to connect with the feelings and emotions of other people?
- Do you see people as dispensable or disposable?
- When you view your business or career, do you feel there is a necessary or needed moral code by which to conduct yourself?
- Do your behaviors and values involve moral considerations of honesty, disclosure, honest communication and right action in which the vulnerabilities of others are not unfairly exploited?
- Is a lack of compassionate self-embrace advising you, constricting you, or crippling you?

The Role of Conscience

Conscience is like a rudder that allows us to assess, dialogue, and course-correct the ship of our life. Not all feelings of guilt are invalid. Some may be divine gifts that allow us to go forward by showing us the need for other actions and behaviors so we can create a very different type of life. Those feelings may be telling us we need to more clearly examine our life course. Such feelings of guilt and shame can become helpful pointers toward a new direction. Conscience takes us to an entirely different place than animals, who operate only out of instinct.

In examining our feelings of guilt, is it possible that those feelings are inspiring us to make positive change? How do we determine when our self-assessments are truly guiding us to a higher level and more beneficial direction and when do thoughts have no truth and value in the mirror of self-reflection?

Shame and guilt can result from an over-developed conscience, shame-based parenting, and community or religious ideas in which the individual felt belittled. Such personal histories may lead to feelings of being imperfect and inadequate to fully claim the status of being human, let alone being a child of God. If these feelings of guilt and shame are not a rudder for self-correction, they can only intensify feelings of unworthiness and lack of deservedness.

We need to gain more clarity about which are valid messages indicating we need to correct our consciousness and our actions. In such a difficulty and dilemma, how do we stabilize these patterns of consciousness so we can stand fully in the sunlight of deservedness? We need to release unhealthy patterns, the self-assault with guilt and shame that constrict our lives.

People vary widely in the development of conscience. An individual may have what we would refer to as an under-developed conscience, while others may have what would be called over-developed conscience. Obviously, an individual with an over-developed conscience is likely to have more difficulties with feelings of guilt, inadequacy and shame. Strong feelings of shame and guilt may also reflect shame-based training as a child. As we have seen, they may also reflect community values in which messages of guilt, shame, and sometimes spiritual inadequacy are part of the culture in which the child has been raised.

Guilt is usually not proportional to the deed, idea, or thought with which it is associated. Our measure of guilt is not an accurate assessment of who we are or what we have done, or failed to do especially in regard to Divine order.

Encouragingly, the experience of guilt can change by redefining the paradigm. If any idea is constantly reinforced with powerful shame, we begin to adopt that as a statement of truth. This statement, reinforced by repetition, creates a distortion that we perceive of as an accurate assessment and validation of who we are.

Inherent Spiritual Truth versus Idea of Indoctrination

Morality exists beyond the dogmas of religion, based instead on intuitive, spiritual knowing tied to spiritual principles of right and wrong. As Lord Krishna tells Arjuna, the embattled soul in *The Bhagavad Gita:* "As unnecessary as a well is to a village on the banks of a river, so unnecessary are all scriptures to someone who has seen the truth." A very different morality involves reinforced learning tells us the right and wrong of a situation through *indoctrinated ideas* based on family, culture, and religious ideology. Conscience is an alignment with Truth from a spiritual perspective. Conscience can also in some cases involve a set of reinforced learned ideas.

Note of clarification: The conscience which is based on a deep, intuitive knowing has its origin in the spiritual truth, divinely reflected. Intuitive knowing has its foundation and existence in the Eternal Self. The conscience of indoctrination develops out of the ideas and behaviors of individuals. The Limited Self develops its conscience structure out of indoctrination by ideas and the external messages from others and the interpretation of ourselves.

Are We Worthy in the Eyes of God?

Are we worthy in the eyes of ourselves? If we hold firmly to the idea that our nature and essence is that of a sinner, unworthy to experience the light of love and the glory of God, we will be blind to who we truly are in our light nature. Our inherent deservedness is based on our nature, the truth and the power of who we really are. Any new exploration and honoring will take us to a greater state of self-realization.

From experience we may vow to extract the knowledge, the determination, and understandings that may allow us to contribute to the good of our lives and those of others. We can channel that knowing into another stream of energy. If we are wasting valuable time, energy, and life force in negative circular energy around guilt, then we have an obligation to ourselves to broaden our concepts and understanding. We have a spiritual obligation to liberate ourselves from destructive chains of past guilt and shame. Therapy may be an invaluable tool in this process. Our new responsibility is to further create and to claim the fields of light.

Redemption from Shame and Guilt by the Law of Grace

There is the grace of God and the truth of that grace is absolute. There is also a law of grace that relates to ourselves, and when we decide and vow to take that negative circular energy and to liberate it in a manner that allows us to be more of a contributor to ourselves, to our own life, and to others, we bestow the law of grace unto ourselves. No mistake is beyond redemption. There is a higher power whose nature is love. We need to expand our loving of self and others to redeem ourselves in the light of new understandings and new motivations for change.

Substitute Negative with Positive/Energized Intention

When we closely examine the repetitive pattern of our own reinforcing thoughts, we can see the bombardment of circular energy that occurs in our own consciousness. Positive affirming statements being substituted for negative self-statements will help break negative circular thought patterns. Affirmations have the power to disrupt and fragment negative circular energy, thus becoming an effective remedy in eliminating negative self-talk. If someone has spent years doubting themselves and affirming their unworthiness, simply stating, "I am loved," will not break the habit. In order to change it, the thought, "I am loved," must be sufficiently infused with energized intention, clearly stated, that it creates vibrational change.

Energized repetition, even if the mind does not accept the truth of the statement being repeated, will nevertheless create dynamic change, in spite of disbelief. State with conviction that which you desire to be expressed. State with conviction and will-charged energy and that which you are desiring shall come into being. The energized statement creates energy fields of movement with or without your belief. If you state truth with proper intention, will-based energy, and an observance of spiritual principles, there will be, with time, manifestation.

Thoughts are Not Neutral

An energy field of thought becomes increasingly invigorated by the energy and emotion that accompany that thought. Thoughts are not neutral. They have the power to be charged with the vibration of positive or negative energy. The thought, "I am not loved," becomes charged with powerful negative energy. Feeling states of sadness and disappointment become infused and entwined with the thought, "I am unloved." That energy operates by the law of magnetism and the law of attraction to seek its own vibrational level. The thought itself creates a state of lack. The thought itself, because it is moving with its own frequency of energy, moves the current of repulsion rather than with the law of attraction in love. The thought of love, depending on the energized belief system, can become a magnet of attraction or the force of repulsion.

Manifesting through the art and technique of visualization also can lead to changes in feeling of deservedness. Powerful, clearly-focused visualizations that involve intention, focused energy and gratitude often have the power to manifest. The successful continuation of demonstrated manifestation may not occur, however, without addressing the core issues that are around the feelings of worthiness and deservedness.

Why We are Deserving and Entitled

Our deservedness is based, first and foremost, on the spiritual nature of man whose origin is from the source of all creation. That truth creates the source of all power for manifestation. Hence you may go deeper into your own nature to utilize principles of manifestation according to spiritual law.

If you wait until you feel fully deserving, or until you feel more entitled to receive, you may wait forever! If you wait for the day of feeling "good enough," "spiritual enough," or "deserving enough" it may never come!

If, on the other hand, you make a claim based on our spiritual deservedness and the right of spiritual entitlement, you will unlock and unleash a new level of energy by which we fuel and fuse our intention with dynamic spiritual energy. It is our right and destiny to access that energy and deepen our relationship with that force of creation.

We were conceived by divinity, created out of divinity, energized by the light of the sun and the stars, and we possess the starlight within ourselves and the star-path homeward. We possess the sunlight of possibilities and the capacity to capture divine emanations and channel the spark of new creation. Our deservedness to receive is not dependent on the opinion of any other, including ourselves. The seed of all creation is within us searching for the sunlight of divine expression once again.

The stream of love and possibilities energized our forms into existence. The stamp of divinity is on our brows. The divinity of all creation is in our hearts. We have power to ignite a thousand suns of possibilities. Our right to receive is based on our profound status of being children of God. Our belief in that God does not change our connection to that light, that source of power, and genesis of love.

 ## Affirmations of Deservedness

For The Gift of Realization
Beloved Heavenly Father,
Beloved Divine Mother,
Friend,
bestow upon me
the gift of realization.
I deserve this rightful gift
for You are mine
and I am Thine.

For Harmony in Deservedness
I act in
harmony with
that God-based
intuition NOW.
I am attuned to right action
with clarity in decision-making.
I am attuned
to the vibration of love.
From that attunement
I deserve
and I am entitled
to all positive manifestation.

For Expansive Entitlement
I am entitled
to the Good.
I am entitled
to the expansive love of God
and the fruits of the earth.

For Deserving All Good
I claim my entitlement.
I deserve
the best of the earth.
I deserve
the divine love of the heavens.
I deserve all that is good,
the highest of the high.

For Divine Claiming
I claim my nature
in claiming the divine light of love.
I claim my nature
in claiming divine friendship.
I claim my nature
in loving.
I claim my nature
in friendship.

For Gratitude in Worthiness
I give thanks for
I am worthy of receiving
God's love,
God's grace.

Chapter Three

Abundance and Prosperity

You are invited on a journey of imagination, visualization, and inner discovery that will lead to greater abundance and prosperity.

As we deepen our awareness of our spiritual essence, we confirm our sense of deservedness. By repeating affirmations of our positive spiritual essence and worthiness to receive, we will increase the positive flow in our life and our access to abundant supply.

Key topics addressed in this chapter:

- Our circumstances are not independent of our consciousness.
- Abundance and prosperity are not tied to material existence alone.
- The Limited Self proceeds from a perception of the finite and lack, and therefore generates and sustains attitudes in consciousness that are tied to limitation. The Limited Self can be a fear-generating mechanism.
- The Eternal Self has no perception of limitation or lack. Its nature is infinite and it operates from the perspective

of the eternal and the infinite. It never participates in lack of consciousness.

Because a change in consciousness is necessary for there to be a change in our material circumstances, this chapter will examine our thought patterns relating to abundance and prosperity. As we think, we manifest. To increase the bountiful flow, we must change the powerhouse of ideas that we claim. A balanced series of activities will lead to this change: self-exploration, positive thinking, meditation, focused visualizations, and spiritual affirmations applied with will-based energy and intention. Imagination is the key. Imagination is the art of etching in the light. Etching in the light with imagination and visualization precedes our potent power to manifest.

Other supports to the manifestation of greater abundance are analysis, problem-solving, and practical approaches such as gathering information, locating resources and networking with others. These techniques will all be discussed in more detail.

Change can only begin with attention to where our consciousness is at this moment in time. Rooting out any tendencies toward self-demeaning attitudes and feelings of futility and hopelessness is necessary if we are to achieve another level of spiritual embrace and attract the abundance we seek. Deservedness issues must be confronted and new thoughts must be formulated into new habits.

All of the wonderful aspects that involve our creativity, our imagination, our ability to visualize, our capacity to affirm are powerful generators of change. But imagination without action will result in stagnation. Visualization without accessing greater knowledge, greater information and pursuing greater understanding will result in ideas floating on clouds, ungrounded by the world under our feet on Earth.

Patient, systematic practice is required, not sporadic efforts with demands for instant results based on magical thinking. No matter how many meditations or affirmations we repeat, castles will not materialize for our enjoyment without our own efforts at construction. These practical techniques involve intention and will-based channeling of energy, analysis and rational thought, along with and creativity.

The Road to Greater Abundance and Prosperity

We also must affirm our prosperity beyond narrow confines and limited ideas of wealth. We cannot define abundance as only material abundance if we are to live in a state of lasting happiness. Do we harbor a consciousness of abundance and reflective gratitude? Is our consciousness tied more to fears of lack and ideas of limited supply? The universe is capable of presenting generous, magnanimous gifts and supplies. If we are to increase the generosity of the universe, the flow is best perceived as coming from a higher universal source. Otherwise the Source becomes named as "chance" or "luck." Ideas that reference "chance" and "luck" may keep us trapped in a limited mental construct tied to the Limited Self. To overcome limited concepts of abundance, we must bombard the Universe, or God, with the **certainty** of response from the Source itself. Anticipating a positive response will open the possibilities of our receiving and increasing our receptivity. Aligned with that Source we cannot fail! Strengthening our connection with that Source is paramount. Training our consciousness into the habit of appreciating the flow of the prosperous good is imperative.

We must examine our thought patterns. Is our consciousness one of lack and insufficiency? Do we have fears about deprivation, limitations, or financial need? Such negative concentration and visualization will generate limited streams of energy. If we shift our consciousness to a view of abundance, prosperity, and expansiveness, we will shift the energy fields in a way that cultivates a boundless crop of positive circumstances and conditions.

There is no magic formula by which dreams can effortlessly materialize abundance and prosperity. However, such dreams can and do materialize with effort, energy, imagination and discipline. As in other areas, an earnest exploration of our habits in consciousness is needed. With that inner voyage of discovery comes an obligation to increase our awareness of outer circumstances and conditions around us. With awareness comes the necessity of organizing, planning, assessing, and evaluating. Developing a plan of movement that allows flexibility and elasticity can positively increase how we participate in a flowing world of wealth, prosperity, and abundance.

Our imagination needs room to soar, but if it is not rooted in the realities of the earth, it will result in flighty ideas, ungrounded circumstances, wishful thinking and fanciful expectations. To offset our deceptive thinking we need to confront our false core ideas and replace them with positive affirmations grounded in truth.

False Core Idea about Abundance and Prosperity

"I am limited in my ability to acquire sufficient abundance and prosperity because of my own inadequacies and the limited material supply."

Such a thought is rooted in any number of false ideas. Which of us has not invoked one of the following ideas and felt justified in doing so without realizing how sabotaging they are? They are the mental and verbal incantations of lack enveloped in deservedness issues. These should bring most people face-to-face with their unconscious thinking:

- My supply and resources are limited.
- I'm unable to achieve my financial goals.
- I'm unable to financially support myself.
- I can't do what I want to do and earn enough money to survive.
- Financial success and creative fulfillment do not go together.
- I have missed my opportunities to be successful. It's too late now.
- I am able to earn only "$$$." (Note how mentally placing a dollar amount around what we earn can become an affirmation in itself in which we are petitioning the universe to limit our supply to that level of money.)
- No matter how hard I work, I can't get ahead financially.
- If I just had more schooling or training, I'd be successful.
- I have bad luck. I never get a real chance to succeed.
- Things never go my way; the world is unfair.
- I will never have enough money to live the life I want.
- I will never get what I truly need and desire.
- Other people always seem to do better than I do.
- It's selfish to expect to prosper.
- To be spiritual is to be in a state of lack. (This thinking may correlate to the idea that God loves the poor more than the rich.)

Why is the core idea false?

The source of abundant supply is limitless and we can always access more of this unlimited supply.

Many people perceive supply as limited because the conditions and socio-economic structure of nations on earth are definitely limiting. Restrictive consciousness is perhaps the most limiting of all conditions that reduce our access in the material realm. We need to invite ourselves to see an expanded vision of possibilities. The physical-material realm does not exist independently from that source of Spirit tied to its creation.

To conceive of prosperity as tied to the possession of a specific object, or class of objects, or a specific financial circumstance, limits the possibility of true abundance. We are surrounded by the abundance of oceanic waters. Financial prosperity is only one stream moving in a limitless universe. Small-minded attitudes regarding Self and supply will create inlets of trapped and confined waters. Our "I-ness" can catch the flow which supplies all life and all universes. History offers plentiful examples of saints and even ordinary people manifesting great material and spiritual riches without tangible earthly cause or source. Jesus produced enough loaves and fishes to feed a multitude from seemingly scant provisions because he tapped into the Divine Source that constantly nurtures us and continues to be accessible to anyone who attunes their consciousness to it.

Whatever our circumstances, we can increase our supply and our contentment and gratitude for our supply. Our consciousness is the fertile ground ever in need of the plowing and re-plowing of ideas and habit tendencies.

Perhaps it is news that abundance and prosperity are not limited to the financial side of life. Our consciousness, ideas, and expectations play an important, if often unobserved, role in the physical circumstances of our lives. We have the power to learn to cultivate an attitude of abundance that allows us to reap the bounty of the earth and the plenty of the heavens.

The idea that material abundance ties primarily, or only, to the operation of the laws of the material world is faulty. The physical-material realm came into being, created from divine idea, distilled into light form. That energized light form enters and solidifies in the physical world. The physical laws of the universe did not create themselves or originate independently from the movement and flow of Spirit. The flow of Spirit forms and creates through the power of imagination. You also have the power to create through imagination. Great inventions originate as seed ideas. How exciting to contemplate the power of imagination to form ideas and images that dance in the light and express its more solid, concrete form in the physical world.

Paramahansa Yogananda makes the point that, "Imagination is not unreal; it is the borderland of what is yet to be real. Everything you imagine can be created by a will that is guided by wisdom." In the Summer 2010 issue of the *Self-Realization* magazine (available from www.yogananda-srf.org), he describes how to materialize cherished dreams and goals.

> "Imagination is a portal through which you can transcend the imposed limitations of this world. All creative persons use this power. With wisdom and will, whatever you can imagine, and continue to imagine can become real. I tell you that things which do not exist now in this world will be created for you. Imagination can be materialized. When you develop spiritually, you

can materialize your thoughts. When you sit still and let your imagination go as far as you can into the realm of your cherished dreams and goals, and if you can hold your mind to one-pointed concentration on the image of what you want to achieve, it will be shown to you in a true-to-life vision. And if you apply strong will power to realizing that vision, ultimately it will manifest— healings can be effected, successes attained, disasters in your environment lessened or avoided, seemingly impossible needs or worthy wishes fulfilled. Your mind united with your soul is such a powerful dynamo of spiritual existence! By increasing the energy of your concentration and calmness, you can consciously realize your connection with the unlimited realm..." (p.7)

You are a creator and a birthmother of creation. Your consciousness infuses seed ideas. These ideas grow through energized intention and the movement of Spirit. With the flow of Spirit the soil of the earth may give birth to the original seed thought. That which exists on the earth, has its origin in the Spirit of the heavens above. All of us have a spiritual responsibility to tend well to the earth and to utilize well the resources that are given to us as caregivers and tillers of the fields. But those fields are also the fields of light. As our consciousness reaches upward, we may access the infinite by the power of thoughts, ideas, and concepts. We can draw from and create with the limitless supply of the universe. Your consciousness can plow those fields of light.

Some key ideas to be considered around prosperity and abundance

- The Source of supply is limitless and infinite.
- Materialization of the supply is initiated through:
    - a. The Genesis of Seed Thoughts. Seed thoughts emerge from Spirit. Conscious thought precedes physical

manifestation of lack or the appearance of abundance. Energized seed thoughts around lack produce lack. Energized seed thoughts around abundance produce abundance. Manifestation follows the flow of consciousness.
b. Imagination/Visualization require dynamic, aligned, will-directed life force.
c. Dynamic Intention in focused, energized concentration is aligned with Spirit. Dynamic intention projects activating energy that manifests as aligned, dynamic willpower. Dynamic intention may be visualized. Dynamic intention may be affirmed.
d. Affirmations become intonations of truth containing the energized source of creation.
e. Analysis and action lay the foundation for new seed thoughts. Acts and actions are necessary for the flow of Spirit to have an avenue to materialize.

The Law of Supply

- The supply of abundance in our life is not separate from our thoughts; feelings of deservedness and entitlement affect our prosperity. For the spiritual law of supply to manifest, clear conceptualization and directed will are necessary.
- The Law of Supply operates through the Law of Magnetism and the Law of Attraction. Our consciousness and mental projections move along energy lines. Those energy lines seek similar vibratory energy. When these energy lines connect or merge with similar energies, they amplify. Amplified energy allows for a greater flow.

- The Law of Supply is operating upon the base of previous actions, activities, and consciousness. Energy has been directed and sent forth from that which has already occurred. That energy is moving in a pattern and cycle of intended completion.
- Previous misuse of the law of supply may be rebalanced by renewed effort and energy with positive intention. Living life with centeredness, equity, fairness and respect for others and the universal flow will generate an energy field by which the future manifestation of the good is being prepared.

Limitation and the Limited Self

The Limited Self perceives prosperity and abundance in a limited, finite fashion. Its vision is earthbound and its tools of measurement and are tied to the scales and measuring stick of financial prosperity on earth. That perception constricts positive flow. Don't underestimate the magnetic power that conscious habits, visualizations, and affirmations may play. Attend to your consciousness in the Now. Your circumstances will always follow the movement of your consciousness. If you will change your circumstances, you must change your consciousness. Manifest prosperity by a prosperity consciousness filled with gratitude. Appreciation for the existing supply increases the supply, allowing us to tap into the endless abundance surrounding our lives.

Is your consciousness centered in prosperity and abundance? Do you have a sense of the power that ever sustains you, manifesting abundant supply in your life? Is your consciousness around your circumstances lacking or is there a feeling and attitude of the bounty of plenty ever manifesting? The supply is limitless. The Source that created all is the power of creation itself. Yet we exist in a physical-material world with physical-material limits. To assume that any level of physical desire will be automatically materialized simply by our wanting, needing, or desiring it, is faulty. Realities and limitations do exist in the physical realm. We live in socio-economic circumstances. Not only are there limitations of the earth, but our greatest limitation is a feeling of estrangement from our higher self, the Eternal Self. Any sense of the earth's inability to supply our needs creates greater feelings of separation and aloneness. This creates both fear and a consciousness of lack.

The consciousness of the Limited Self operates in habitual, ego-based patterns of thinking. It operates from finite ideas of limitation with insufficient awareness of the possibilities of manifestation through divine laws. Most of us have such an insufficient awareness. Ideas around our entitlement to receive, right to access and materialize prosperity directly influence the material manifestation in our lives. As we believe we deserve, we shall further create and attract to us those conditions and those circumstances. We must visualize receiving and practice gratitude for the abundance that we receive. As we think, we become. And as we project, we manifest. If we increase our awareness of our spiritual essence, we will increase our feelings of deservedness. As we affirm our positive spiritual essence and our worthiness to receive by the use of affirmations, we will increase the positive flow in our life and our access to abundant supply.

Whatever our financial circumstances, it is our mental habits and attitudes, positive or negative, that bring lack or abundance. As our efforts to align the Limited Self and the

Eternal Self become more successful, we finally come to access more of the universe's supply. The universal supply will begin to manifest itself by our efforts in changing our thought patterns related to our perception of ourselves. Self-perception fosters and creates greater access to abundant supply. The power of Spirit to create, to manifest, and to materialize in harmonious cooperation continues to underlie the foundation of our existence. Each of us has the power to access that indelible power of Spirit.

Analysis and action

The idea that life will take care of itself and the flow will stream by the act of visualization is unrealistic. This view diminishes the power of man as a dynamic player: man in the act of thinking, man in the act of visualizing, and man in the act of acting—generating, solving, creating, and manifesting. Too many self-help perspectives attempt to engage the imagination and the creative process, but the creative process un-channeled and under-directed by the power of will, will yield floating, formless ideas that never achieve concrete materialization.

Whatever your present circumstances, you have the power to change them. An important step in creating change is to analyze those current circumstances. Look at your situation realistically. Analyze it clearly. Engage in concrete analysis and problem-solving. Your ability to problem-solve, as well as to analyze, is also one of God's gifts.

Only when you honestly face where you are in any given situation can you allow imagination and creativity to be a wondrous part of the solution. Do not depend on wishful thinking; such thinking is stagnant energy, lacking the will and logic to find solutions and to apply practical plans and strategy. Too many people go to imagination, wishful thinking, and hope as the primary remedy for their circumstances; the mind's powers to concentrate and to develop solutions and strategies is ignored. Yet rational thought is the foundation of effective problem-solving. Analysis and information-gathering precede the creative process. Manifestation requires both the mental and the physical or practical realms.

When those realms are disconnected or separate from one another, they will not yield consistent results. To imagine or visualize abundance without analyzing present circumstances and forming an action plan is unlikely to produce results. An action plan involves an analysis of circumstances, a goal of problem-solving, and a list of the main steps to be achieved in order to create forward movement. A solid action plan is an excellent path toward a greater flow of good in your life. Too many books emphasize the power of the mind to imagine, without sufficiently emphasizing the significant practical aspect of will-directed activity and corresponding action. You could visualize affluence, abundance, and prosperity every day, yet if you do not take action, or your action is scattered and unfocused, there will be little momentum toward materializing what you desire.

In your action plan build in small goals that you can monitor, assess and see results. Being able to see some positive results, however small, will reinforce your ability to plan.

Man is a dynamic activator with the power to set in motion actions which birth creation. The power to imagine and the power to act are the twofold aspects that allow true creation. To be willing to apply logic and analysis in the design of specific plans and goals allows Spirit to pave the roadway toward solutions.

When you analyze your situation, you then can activate energy that may be used to apply dynamic willpower. Dynamic willpower is energized will. Energized will draws from the life force and the limitless sea of Spirit. Cut away the expectation that, if you desire enough, the universe will present your dreams come true to you. Instead, know that you were made with the power to create and to concentrate your force in directed thrust. Dynamic willpower is the thrust and generator of possibilities. It is a necessary prerequisite for manifestation to occur.

Discernment is also important in creating a greater abundant flow. The rational, analytical part of the self merges with the intuitive, reflective capacity—the left brain with the right—in order to produce true discernment. Acting with discernment prevents rash decisions, wishful thinking, unrealistic expectations and the pitfalls of foolhardiness. A discerning nature proceeds confidently toward goals that are in tune with Divine truth and true self-interest. This results in abundance at the highest levels, benefiting not only oneself but others.

Introspection Exercise

- Analyze your present circumstances.
- Analyze your financial conditions at present.
- Analyze the work that you are doing.
- Analyze five strengths in your skill sets.

Then give yourself the freedom to write down whatever thoughts come to you in terms of what you want. All people have skills. What are yours? Are you good with people? Do you possess mechanical or electronic talents? Do you see yourself as having verbal skills of persuasion, or the ability to influence others? Is there a way to employ any of your skills more usefully? Is there a way you could experiment with transferring some of your skills to a different field or job in a way that would not jeopardize your present financial circumstances? Is there an area of interest or creativity that you have always wanted to explore? Do new educational fields, trade skills or abilities beckon?

- Analyze the facts and factors in your life that are holding you back from new areas of exploration.
- Two obstacles that prevent people from trying something new are the fear of failure and the fear of success. If you can step away from that paradigm and see yourself as an adventurer, would that allow you more freedom to pursue new activities, new interests and financial horizons?
- Analyze your goals and realistic ways to achieve them.
- If you feel you have an interest in a specific subject, or the possibility of a new career, can you acquire more experience and expertise in smaller increments rather than proceeding in a way that may create enormous risks to you and those dependent on you? Simply transferring skills does not automatically result in enough experience to justify changing careers or entering into new enterprises. Because change can be destabilizing professionally, analyzing and implementing smaller steps towards a change can create a bridge over which you may be able to walk towards new opportunities in career and creativity. Pursuing new interests part-time may allow

you to create enough of a foundation that, with time, you may transition into a more positive work situation.
- Analyze the areas which you wish to pursue.

It is not necessary for you to have all of the answers, but you must become more proficient in asking questions. Be willing to assimilate, **analyze, activate** and **act** on those areas of career and creative interests. Acquiring more information or knowledge is not time lost, but time gained in a new level of mastery. People often feel that if another endeavor, enterprise or career is God's will for them, that the road will be smooth and effortless. Yet the abilities to make an effort, apply will, and energize our creative vision are gifts that we have inherited from the Divine Source Itself. The development of these attributes and skills is often part of our empowerment and divine claiming.

If you desire to increase your financial flow, you have to examine and understand your habit patterns in consciousness. You also need to understand patterns and trends in the work and financial worlds. You will become empowered by understanding more of who you are *and* by increasing your understanding of economic principles.

Expansion and expansiveness come from increasing your understanding of yourself and your world. Both elements are needed because if your consciousness is restricted around deservedness issues, no matter what financial flow comes to you, you will find a way to end up feeling you are materially deficient. If you attend to your habit patterns in consciousness and improve self-understanding, but have no understanding of the times and changes in the world of work and technology, you may encounter problems. If you stay inattentive to practical matters, you will not waste time, effort, and resources in dead-ends. It is important to pay attention to projected trends, upcoming changes, and advances in technology. An expansive consciousness may not be sufficient in itself to counter a lack of practical information about the physical-material world in which you live.

The good news is that the work of self-knowing leads in the end to joy in self-knowing. In that joy you will experience the expansiveness of yourself. Perhaps you will even experience the expansiveness of the universe and touch the face of the Infinite. If you increase self-knowing, you will see the universal flow that underlies all life, all worlds, as well as the universe of your own consciousness. You cannot increase your self-knowing without that invitation to joy and expansiveness. Abundant participation and revealing resources unfold before you, seemingly as a magic carpet of possibilities. That which feels like the burden of self-exploration and self-discovery, in the end, gives you wings to fly and a limitless universe with abundant opportunities in which to soar.

Become a Master of Your Consciousness

If you are not a master of your circumstances, you can become increasingly a master of your consciousness. Greater mastery of your consciousness will, in the end, always change your circumstances. The force of all creation is in residence within you. No matter how foreign that concept may seem to you, increased penetration through interiorized consciousness (meditation in the stillness) will allow you to penetrate the wealth of all knowing. You will also gain access to the streams of abundance that underlie all creation. Limitless supply is available to those who increasingly become aware of their Eternal

Self and strive to remain unfettered by the limited consciousness of the Limited Self.

If you experience perceptions of limitation, increasing your alignment to Spirit will increase your perception of the abundant flow of the universe. The law of supply operates through expansive and magnanimous spiritual laws. All spiritual law is founded in the vibration of love. Love is the essence of all and permeates all creation. Man's opportunity and invitation is to participate more in that vibration of love and come to experience that joy unending.

Unlock Your Mind Power

It becomes difficult to affirm greater prosperity if you are in a circumstance of dwindled resources or reduced faith. If you believe that life's blocked opportunities and reversals have created a constricted and limited life, you may find it difficult and unrealistic to focus on the positive. Also, you may feel it's natural to keep reviewing your present situation from the perspective of lack. To continuously re-energize a lack-centered consciousness will send forth negative energy from those seed thoughts. These thoughts are powerful generators of your future conditions. You, in the present, are creating the conditions that you will inhabit in the future. Ideas have power to germinate circumstances. Ideas are not neutral. Ideas are an energized force in creation.

While it may be helpful to assess how you have reached your present circumstances, to obsess or ruminate over that which has already occurred can be counterproductive. Excessive negative re-plays restrict flow and reinforce a mindset that views yourself in diminished perspective.

There exists a potent force of power in the universe that operates by the law of magnetic attraction to create either greater lack or greater abundance and prosperity.

You have the power to unlock your mind! Your gift at image projection by imagination and the thrust of dynamic will expand as you regularly review your own consciousness. You are a creator! You are a light generator! And you have the power to access the energy of the universe and the power of the sun!

Faith alone, simply believing in the emergence of new, positive circumstances, without your own energy and initiative, will yield only disappointing results. God's ability to assist you is amplified when you use your own directed, will-based energy. Employing your own talents, abilities, and resources will attract, by the law of magnetism, new opportunities and more positive circumstances. Many people believe that positive change will result from sufficient faith or sufficiently strong appeals born of desperation. Those appeals may become new affirmations of negativity.

Even with sufficient faith, as well as effort and application, people may remain in situations of challenge. Do negative circumstances mean that some people are less favored by God? Does prosperity mean another person is more favored by God? An excellent commentary on this idea is to be found in Weber's, *The Protestant Ethic and the Spirit of Capitalism.*

The power of positive affirmations to affect change is not tied to faith or belief. The power of positive affirmations is tied to the repetition of energized spiritual truth that affirms the greater good. Man in divine cooperation, in ever-greater attunement, then accesses more of the divine force in dynamic materialization and in internal participation.

Faith should be anchored in divine truth and spiritual law, if it is to be sufficiently powerful to generate change. Energized repetition of ideas, either negative or positive, creates a dynamic, potent force of creation in the universe. Yet we doubt that we are potent creators of our own conditions and circumstances. We look to become more faithful and believe that our power resides in faith alone. Such thoughts may minimize the dynamic thrust of ideas, imagination, and creative participation with the larger force of All.

Introspection Opportunity

Summon new levels of manifestation and the appearance of abundance and prosperity in your life. You can make them APPEAR.

- **A**nalyze
    a. Analyze your present conditions and circumstances.
    b. Analyze your prosperity consciousness. (Do you believe you have a right to prosper?)
    c. Analyze whether you have given yourself *permission* to prosper and access limitless supply. Do you feel that you do not have a right to succeed and prosper? What is the origin of those thoughts and feelings? Do you carry deservedness issues? Your dynamic intention must first be fueled by your permission to prosper. Permission itself gives a powerful momentum to will. Permission unleashes and directs will-based energy.

- **P**rioritize
    a. What areas need to be changed?
    b. What positive areas could be further expanded?
    c. Create a list of areas that need to be changed, indicating some system of immediate change, and then the change that has less urgency. Everything else will fall into the middle category. You might list "1" as the most urgent and "3" as the least urgent; everything else is "2." Start with level "1." Then prioritize. Do not begin the changes on the "2" list until all of number "1" is completed.
- **P**erseverance

  Perseverance involves repeated willed activity toward a specific goal or specified direction. Without perseverance there will be minimal creation and action. The act of volition, or movement, is driven by perseverance. Creativity is ignited by the movement of action, ideas, activities. The more that an idea, steps, or an activity is refortified and energized by perseverance, the more will is focused and expanded. Also, the power of creativity is further expanded, as well as your ability to achieve mastery of goals.
- **E**nergize your dynamic intention into purpose-driven activity. Activity needs to be activated by imagination, visualization, and a statement of intention in order for you to be a true co-creator in an abundant exchange with the universe.
- **A**ction is necessary. No change can occur without a decision to take action. Otherwise, dreams remain dreams, and visualized scenes never manifest. Imagination without action limits the possibility of

significant change and movement, keeping both only in the realm of possibility. From your change list, select any item that allows you to make change by taking action. Add to your list what your fears are about what will happen if you initiate change. Fears create stagnation and paralysis of dynamic will. Fear-based actions cripple dynamic flow and creativity and thus constrict abundance. About fears: Name them! Claim them! Eliminate them!

- **R**esearch. Be willing to investigate and explore information about areas in which you are interested. If you are considering new endeavors, or new business projects, or new ways of marketing an established product, explore relevant data. Insufficient information may limit your ability to go forward. Add creativity to your exploration of relevant information and processes.

Let us keep the knowledge base that we possess and invigorate it with new information and be willing to listen to input from experts. Let us be willing to pay attention to new trends, ideas which have a solid knowledge base. We can take those ideas and allow them to become incubated with creativity and imagination before the movement and motion of action. "Magical thinking" based on desires will not be more powerful than the infusion of mental constructs based on concrete realities currently in motion and operation.

Again, we see that the joining of consciousness, ideas, imagination and visualization with solid analysis, information, and adequate research, can produce positive results and new possibilities.

To create new levels of resources and access greater abundance and prosperity, use analysis, permission to prosper, dynamic intention, and dynamic visualization, as well as affirmations, combined with the habit of gratitude. With gratitude, act *as if divine manifestation has already materialized.*

Your attitudes impact your prosperity

There is a direct relationship between your attitudes and that which is attracted to you through the law of magnetism and attraction.

Attitudes to cultivate:
1. The attitude of gratitude and appreciation.
2. The attitude of thankfulness.
3. A positive attitude towards the prosperity of others.

Your attitudes are the road upon which prosperity and abundance travel. Your attitudes project dynamic energy, and can attract circumstances by the law of magnetism. Your circumstances can be altered by paying close attention to the habit patterns in your thoughts.

Introspection

- Write down your attitudes and ideas around how you see prosperity and abundance in your life. Gaining clarity about how your individualized thought patterns cluster into broader attitudes will give you specific target areas to address.
- Write down what you say to yourself when good fortune and prosperity suddenly occurs.
- Write down what you say to yourself when unexpected financial reverses, or states of lack, dominate your life. This will help you gain insight into your attitudes and

thoughts. Are you a dynamic co-Creator or a passive recipient of luck or chance circumstances. If you cannot analyze how you usually perceive and inner dialogue around your circumstances, you will find it more difficult to consciously change toward a more positive flow. You will also have difficulty identifying how changes of habit, as well as techniques such as affirmations, can help create such change in your life.

The Attitude of Gratitude and Appreciation

You are part of a bigger picture. When you begin to see yourself as a part of the stream of the good by which the divine flow moves, you will further access not only your own supply but more of an ability and willingness to supply to others. When you mistakenly see all that you have as coming from your own efforts, or your power to make others supply your wants, needs, and desires, then you may further tighten your grip into a greater fear of lack. Your efforts have been important and your participation has been vital to that which has manifested in your life. That which exists now did not originate in a vacuum. But heightening your awareness that you are part of a larger flow of limitless abundance will increase your capacity to experience the increased flow in your consciousness, your circumstances and relationships with others.

Whatever your present level of flow, still practice the habits of gratitude and appreciation. Cultivate the habit of gratitude along with practicing more the **feeling state** of appreciation. To feel more gratitude, bring to your mind, from past memories, a situation or circumstance in which you felt grateful. Try to remember the scene and the feeling state that accompanied that. Keep revolving that theme and that feeling state in your mind. As you are in greater attunement with that feeling state, try to review your present circumstances. To the best of your ability attach that same feeling state to situations and experiences in the Now. That technique will increase your ability to feel gratitude in a broader circle of circumstances. Also, even if you do not feel particularly grateful, simply repeat, "I am grateful, I am thankful, I am a receiver of the good." Repeating that affirmation will increase your ability to feel gratitude.

By cultivating attitudes of gratitude and appreciation, the universe will respond. Your positive flow of appreciation will generate, like a magnet, a divine response. Along with cultivating appreciation, also cultivate the habit of saying "thank you" to the Divine Source. Change your relationship to being a true co-creator with the divine. See yourself as being abundantly supplied and abundantly supplying.

Appreciation and gratitude will continue to increase the greater possibilities of positive materialization in your life. Visualizing, affirming, and practicing statements of ever-greater faith in possibilities are powerful tools by which the new manifests. Being proactive in changing your consciousness empowers your life.

As your consciousness cultivates, your circumstances manifest. Proceed as if you have the power and the right of access to the limitless good of the earth. Proceed as if God will move in divine response to your intention. Proceed as if you will be successful in penetrating into that vast reservoir of abundant supply. Proceed as if success will be yours, victory and prosperity will be yours. And so shall it be.

Practice the habit of thankfulness

There is a distinction between thankfulness and gratitude. Gratitude is a feeling state and thankfulness is the expression of that state in words or thought. Thankfulness opens the road of supply. To be thankful is to express the feeling of gratitude. Thankfulness takes form in words sent into the universe by verbal expression or by conscious thought and mental intention. Thankfulness is an act of volition directed by will. Will-directed energy intensifies and expands by repetition.

Gratitude, by repetition, also generates a powerful magnetized energy into the universe. It is the sentiment of the heart. Both gratitude and thankfulness project into the universal flow. Practice both mentally and verbally by giving thanks for the small, daily indications of the good, the positive, and the spiritual blessings in your life.

Giving mental and verbal thanks for the blessings you are receiving brings the two selves into greater alignment and opens your relationship to the spiritual source. By the act of thankfulness you will train your mind to look at that which is supplied to you as coming from a reservoir of limitless supply. Change your relationship by experiencing the power of talking to, dialoging with, and expressing thankfulness to the Creator of All. In gratitude we expand our participation with the Divine. In thankfulness we project that love and gratitude to the Eternal Source.

A positive attitude towards the prosperity of others

The highest intention as a human and divine player is to facilitate good on behalf of others. This is because we are all one through our common spiritual source. The other is you, and you are the other. That is the secret behind many secrets. The act of well-wishing and enthusiastic support for the good in other people's lives will create a harmonious flow for yourself and for others. You will have greater access to the good and to abundance based on a true spiritual foundation.

Guard against lack-centered attitudes and jealousy towards the good fortune of others. That is an attitude of the Limited Self. It is contrary to the knowing of the Eternal Self. That same source that is plowing the fertile field of an expansive, abundant universe for others is tilling the soil from which you receive from the great harvest.

Make a God contract – be a contributor

A principle in tithing, based on sound spiritual principles, involves returning in some form a portion of that which has been given to you. This act acknowledges the Source that is beyond yourself. In this act you recognize that what you have received has been provided by a force beyond your own efforts. Your effort can access the flow of life, but it is not the source of the flow of all life. To access the flow is to access the source of all which is in divine participation with you.

Be a contributor! Make a commitment that is real and solid to return part of that which is given to you in some way. To contribute financially, or to contribute with time, effort, or mentoring, allows you to claim and empower more of your life by participating with others, while creating greater alignment between the Limited Self and the Eternal Self.

Make a contract with yourself. What are you willing to give on a weekly, monthly, or yearly basis that can create a greater flow to another or others? Your giving is the vibration of love that has been given to you and is redistributed by the kindness of your heart. That kindness cooperates with the universe. Your acts of kindness create an expansive flow of generosity that creates more abundance and continuing generosity.

Mentoring – Give the gift of yourself

In addition to the principle of tithing, the principle involved in mentoring offers a sacred opportunity to nurture and nourish others. Mentoring allows talents, attributes and areas of potential growth to be cultivated, encouraged, and directed. It requires proceeding with intention and will-directed activity towards increasing the beneficial good to another. Through the act of mentoring, you can nurture the potential of another, helping that sacred flame of inner light that wishes to expand in the light of day. Volunteering in groups, organizations, or activities that are community-based can be another way of giving back in gratitude for that which has been given to you.

Introspection

Examine closely your own attitudes around giving.
- Do you see the act of giving to another as taking or denying yourself, or depleting the possibility of your receiving adequate supply? Are you giving to another in a manner that may make them feel indebted or obligated?
- Do you give out of a sense of duty? Do you feel your heart is restrictive in resenting giving to another? If you see your security as simply tied to your own efforts and limitations, you may feel anxious about sharing. If you have been, at times, in places of great challenges, you may have fears about letting go of that which you feel is your security. While it is not wise to give unrealistically, still you have the capacity out of your resources, finances, or time and energy to find a way to contribute. You can expand your participation with the light of others. Your light in sharing will cast a new glow of possibility and may even light the pathway ahead for them.
- Assess how you give. What form does it take? Are there ways you can expand as a contributor? Write down your giving strategies.
- Assess and analyze if there is a way to increase your giving without creating undo feelings of obligation. If a gift makes another feel oppressed by the obligation, it loses part of its meaning. Some gifts may best be made anonymously; other times that is not the case. The most important thing is to examine your own heart and continue to work with your own attitudes. That which is given should not be seen as simply coming from you, but

from the flow of life and the universe of love. Your act of generosity continues the flow of God's generosity to you. Be a dispenser of the good, knowing you are a conduit of the force of light and love.

Introspection Opportunity: Abundance and Prosperity

Your ideas impact abundance and prosperity in your life. Write down the answers to these questions:

- Early in life, did you hear positive messages spoken about your vibrant future and your abilities and capabilities to succeed? Were specific talents, aptitudes, and abilities emphasized, encouraged and praised? Do you feel you heard that your abilities and talents would result in financial security, abundance, and continuous supply?
- What is the content of your inner dialogue around your right to prosper? Do you repeat sentences you heard your mother or father say about your potential success or failure?
- What do you say to yourself about your entitlement or deservedness to achieve prosperity?
- In your mind, is the concept of abundance tied exclusively or primarily to financial success? Do your ideas around abundance encompass other areas of your life? What are those areas?
- What is your assessment about your ability to access the flow of abundance now and in your future endeavors? How do you assess your personal ability to experience or manifest prosperity on a daily basis? What are your future projections?

- Do you feel that desiring abundance and prosperity is selfish and egotistical or perhaps, greedy?
- Do you have a conflict that views prosperity and abundance as inharmonious with spiritual desires? Do you feel that "Good people are not rich people?"

Have you given yourself permission to succeed?

Your thoughts and ideas around prosperity and abundance impact the flow of abundance and prosperity in your life. Prosperity and abundance are not limited to ideas of financial and material success alone, but rather to ideas of giving yourself permission to access the supply of the universe in all aspects. There is a Source that supplies. There is a Source that creates and continues to create. There is a Source that manifests and continues to manifest. You are part of that Source: creating, accessing, and manifesting in the physical-material realm.

Our ideas can limit, restrict and constrict the flow of abundance that comes to us. Another personal tendency may be to cast fear-bound anxieties into mental projections of the future. Sometimes we worry in advance about our future although we will never meet those circumstances. Anxiety and fear become the screen upon which the future image is cast. A more desirable feeling to cultivate is **calmness, centeredness,** and **certainty** of God's ability to provide flow for you. If you are projecting fear, anxiety, and trepidation into visualized images of the future, you constrict the flow of the good and change that which is attracted to you. That feeling state, alone, has the power to penetrate into the process of visualization, which then energizes the negative vision. If your overall imagining of your future state of affairs is charged with negativity, how is it that a few minutes a day imagining prosperity will counter that force field of energy? That is why introspection, analyzing consciousness, and the systematic practice of working with interior calmness, visualization, and affirmation are needed to counter our negative habits.

Before you practice visualizations around abundance and prosperity, first practice imagining yourself in scenes and experiences that brought you great joy in the past. See yourself in those settings, relaxed, peaceful, and calm, as well as joyous. Use your gift of memory and imagination to embellish peaceful and joy-felt states. Intensify those remembered states of consciousness by activating evermore your gifts of imagination. Relax and pay attention to your breath patterns and feel as if you are riding the waves of incoming and outgoing breath in divine centeredness. Preferably use a quality meditation technique. If you do not have an established meditation routine or technique, you may want to pursue techniques by contacting Self-Realization Fellowship. (Self-Realization Fellowship, 3880 San Rafael Avenue, Los Angeles California 90065-3219 or online at www.yogananda-srf.org)

If you practice visualizing a prosperous and abundant future, center your energy in a place of calmness. With relaxed visualization, project positive images. Let your feelings mirror the image of prosperity and abundance! Respond with gratitude and thankfulness at being a recipient of the bounty of the earth.

To project fear energy into future imagined scenes dilutes the possibility of feeling safe and secure in the Now. How many of us have known people who survived desperate financial circumstances? Some of those individuals were forever corralled in that state of fear, where the fear of lack became their only reality no matter how much abundance or prosperity would later surround them. The experience of lack and the fear of lack left them constricted without a new vision or dream, thus impairing their ability to access, appreciate, and give gratitude for positive changes in their circumstances. The terror of lack blocked their ability to experience gratitude and thankfulness for their present life.

More on Introspection – Career and Finances:

Let us take the thought, "no matter how hard I work, I probably will only be able to generate a yearly income of X." Give yourself the opportunity to experiment with this idea to become more aware of your own process of inner dialogue.

- What do you feel you will earn this year? Write that amount down on a piece of paper, based on your present circumstances.
- What do you estimate you will earn annually in the next couple of years? Ask yourself the question, "Do I ever participate in internal dialogue that says, no matter how hard I work, I probably will never be able to earn over XXX in any given year?" If you discover that you are entering into this limiting, internal dialogue, it is critical to see that this thought has become an energized affirmation. That energized affirmation is limiting your flow and your entitlement to prosper. The thought of a capped amount is broadcast to the universe saying: "Divine Source, please limit my supply. Make it possible that I only earn X dollars a year." By repeating this idea, materialization or manifestation at a physical-material level will follow. But if new ideas of abundance are

sufficiently charged with dynamic intention and will-based action, the law of attraction will bring a magnetism of prosperity.

Remember that ideas of abundance, prosperity, and greater access are blueprints of creation, just as ideas of a cap on abundance or limit to prosperity can lead to a manifestation of lack. Often, it is not circumstances or others blocking our prosperity, but ourselves. Is it possible that you may be participating in a way that inadvertently blocks the flow and access to that stream of prosperity? We constrict the flow of supply in our own personal, non-affirming dialogue.

Repetition of energy in the light will, in the end, become the materialized aspect. The power of negative self-affirming exists whether we are aware of it or not. Any internalized, negative dialogue over time becomes a concrete negative affirmation, counter-productive to all.

You cannot change your present conditions without changing your attitudes around your circumstances. Even then, your previous thoughts and actions have set in motion events still in the process of coming to meet you. You are not a prisoner of that reality. Your ultimate freedom comes from understanding that your thoughts, ideas, and self-dialogue can align with the higher self of greater illumination. Remember, it is the Limited Self that participates in ideas of worthiness and dreams the dreams of non-entitlement. The Limited Self punishes, judges and chastises the self around the potential rights of entitlement. The Eternal Self is radiant with the truth that you are one with that Eternal Source unable to be truly disconnected from the limitless supply of the universe. Only your mind, thoughts, and ideas filter the streaming light of possibilities and prosperity.

Emanations of new forms take shape as your mind wraps itself around a new flower and fragrance of possibility.

Visualize and affirm abundance

See yourself, visualize yourself in abundant circumstances.

The repetition and restatement of any affirmation creates an energy further empowered by visualization. Mentally practice seeing yourself in abundant circumstances. As you visualize, combine the image of abundance with powerful words affirming the truth of the dynamic supply of the universe. The universe is limitless! The universe is expanding in its own possibilities of creation! The divine is a director of creation, but we are divine creators in combined co-creation with that Dynamic Source. Your feelings, at some level, of not being good enough to adequately receive abundance, prosperity, and expansive generosity from the Divine comes from a constricted view of your worth. The spark of divinity resides in your nature. Part of the creator of all is resident within, co-creating with you in a dance of light and possibility. When did you start limiting your dreaming by a lesser vision of yourself? Ignite the flame of possibility that is within you! Flame the spark of divinity that is in divine cooperation with the truest desires of your heart.

The Divine Source is igniting possibilities and realities of ever-greater prosperity and abundance. The spark of God is co-creating with you in the divine expression of greater flow, greater light, and ever-greater prosperity and abundance. Light is your nature, love is your nature, and the Divine is manifesting in the name of that Light, and in the name of that Love. Abundance and prosperity are yours! The limitless universe awaits greater connection with you! Abundance and prosperity are your due. Mine, with one-pointed focus, the riches of the earth while the stars share their diamond brilliance. Be a star catcher and a stargazer. Treasures await!

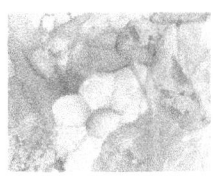

Affirmations for Abundance and Prosperity

<u>For Abundance</u>
I give thanks for
I am a magnet of success.
Doors of opportunity
are opening wide for me NOW.

<u>For Success through God</u>
I give thanks for
I am a magnet of success.
God is opening doors
of opportunity NOW.

<u>For Harmony and Attunement to Limitless Supply</u>
I am in harmonious balance
With the Divine and the Universe.
That Divine Source
is materializing ever-greater abundance,
prosperity and resources in my life NOW.
I attune to the Divine Source
in harmonious co-creation.
I am receiving from the limitless supply
of the Divine and the Universe NOW."

<u>For Abundance in the Father</u>
My Father and I are One.
All things whatsoever the Father hath are mine."
                              (Source: John 16:15)

<u>For Material Abundance Manifesting</u>
I give thanks for the great material abundance
manifesting in my life NOW.
Prosperity is my due!
Wealth is my claim!

For Material Abundance through Creativity
Divine creativity
is expanding
in amplified form
within me NOW.
Creativity is a conduit
for my financial prosperity
manifesting NOW.

For Creation for Within
The force of all creation is resident within me.
I am grateful.
I am thankful.
I am a receiver of the good.

For Participating in the Flow of Love
I am a dispenser of the good.
I am a participant in the universal
flow of love.

For Abundance through Creativity
Abundance and prosperity
are manifesting
through my creative endeavors
of will,
imagination,
and dynamic intention.

For Thankfulness
I give thanks for the great materialization
of abundance and prosperity
manifesting in my life NOW.

www.ingramcontent.com/pod-product-compliance
Lightning Source LLC
Chambersburg PA
CBHW022305060426
42446CB00007BA/598